Modernizing Medical Research: AI and Medical Records

Bill Inmon

Dave Rapien

Dr Sylvia Sydow

Technics Publications
SEDONA, ARIZONA

115 Linda Vista, Sedona, AZ 86336 USA
https://www.TechnicsPub.com

Edited by Steve Hoberman
Cover design by Lorena Molinari

All rights reserved. No part of this book may be reproduced or transmitted in any form or by any means, electronic or mechanical, including photocopying, recording or by any information storage and retrieval system, without written permission from the publisher, except for brief quotations in a review.

The authors and publisher have taken care in the preparation of this book but make no expressed or implied warranty of any kind and assume no responsibility for errors or omissions. No liability is assumed for incidental or consequential damages in connection with or arising out of the use of the information or programs contained herein.

All trade and product names are trademarks, registered trademarks, or service marks of their respective companies and are the property of their respective holders and should be treated as such.

Without in any way limiting the author's exclusive rights under copyright, any use of this publication to "train" generative artificial intelligence (AI) technologies to generate text is expressly prohibited. The author reserves all rights to license uses of this work for generative AI training and the development of machine learning language models.

First Printing 2025

Copyright © 2025 by Bill Inmon, David Rapien, and Dr Sylvia Sydow

ISBN, print ed.   9781634627153
ISBN, Kindle ed.   9781634627160
ISBN, PDF ed.   9781634627177

Library of Congress Control Number: 2025934621

Contents

Preface 1

Acknowledgments 5

Chapter 1: The Need for Modernizing Medical Research 7
    Unlocking the treasure trove 9
    Research and medical records 10
    The challenges of looking at a population 11
    Text as an obstacle 13
    Textual disambiguation 16
    A step by step approach 16
    Heuristic analysis 17
    From ah? to aha! 18
    The need for speed 20
    Obstacles to achieving speed of analysis 21
    Autonomy of analysis 23
    In summary 23

Chapter 2: Taxonomies and Ontologies 25
    Taxonomies 27
        Relevance 28
        Completeness of the taxonomy 29
        Unique identification 29
        Medical taxonomies 30
        How are taxonomies used? 31
        A real world, external foundation 33
        The size of the taxonomy 33
        Periodic maintenance 34
    Ontologies 34
    In summary 35

Chapter 3: Ingesting Text — 37
Privacy and the law — 37
Storage media — 39
Images — 39
Medical record selection — 40
Medical record structure — 41
Managing volumes of data — 44
Different data formats — 45
- The Internet — 46
- In print — 47
- Spreadsheets — 48
- On a voice recording — 49
- Email — 50

In summary — 51

Chapter 4: Research Journals and Clinical Trials — 53
Medical journals — 53
Clinical trials and patient records — 54
Text and clinical trials — 55
The structure of the study — 57
The number of studies/clinical trials — 59
Reading the entire document — 60
Resolving terminology differences — 61
In summary — 62

Chapter 5: Unification of Text — 63
Encoding — 66
Measurement — 67
Language — 68
Common structure — 69
Spelling — 70
Grouping similar objects — 70
Acronyms — 71
Homographs — 72
Calculations — 73

Further elucidation _____ 74
Formatting adjustments _____ 74
Different name for the same object _____ 75
In summary _____ 76

Chapter 6: Building the Database _____ 77
The basic interface _____ 78
Simple questions _____ 79
The Datavox database _____ 81
Adjusting the vocabulary _____ 81
A closer look at the output data _____ 83
In summary _____ 85

Chapter 7: Exploration _____ 87
Exploration and clinical trials _____ 88
Computer systemization _____ 89
The potential of no resolution _____ 92
Lessons learned from an exploration _____ 97
Different approaches to exploration _____ 98
Scatter diagrams _____ 99
Correlation _____ 100
A Pearson coefficient matrix _____ 102
The need for speed _____ 104
In summary _____ 105

Chapter 8: Analytics _____ 107
Many forms of analysis _____ 108
Operating from the same database _____ 109
Textual database versus a structured database _____ 109
Different types of analytical tools _____ 112
   Spreadsheet data analysis – Excel _____ 115
   Genai based query suite – Thoughtspot _____ 118
   Knowledge graphs – Neo4j _____ 122
   Dashboards – Tableau _____ 125

Chapter 9: Analytics on Structured and Textual Data — 129
Analytics in the structured environment — 129
Analytics on both structured and textual data — 130
Different organizations of data — 131
Intersecting data — 134
Connectors — 135
Stable/unstable connectors — 136
Types of relationships — 137
   No relationship — 137
   Universal relationship — 138
   Direct relationship — 140
   Indirect relationship — 141
   Classification-based relationship — 142
Different connections — 142
An example of blending textual and structured data — 144
In summary — 146

Chapter 10: The Analytical Lifecycle — 147
A "normal" procedure — 148
Flexibility — 151
Length of time — 152
Speed of textual ETL — 154
Attitude — 156
Reconsidering the study — 156
In summary — 157

Index — 159

Preface

Dave and I are not medical professionals. Do not take medical advice from us. However, we are seasoned information and data professionals, and very familiar with medical practices and medical information.

There is a distinction between having expertise in medicine and having expertise in medical information. We do not fit the first category, but we definitely fit the second category.

When it comes to medical advice, we depend on Dr Sylvia Sydow, whose medical advice and treatment are invaluable.

This book describes new and intriguing ways to enhance medical research. This book is not a criticism of medical research. Instead, this book covers how to improve existing methods of medical research. The techniques are complementary to existing research practices. In no way do they replace existing approaches to research.

On a personal basis, I am a big fan of existing medical practices. Had it not been for medicine and doctors, I would not be here today. I owe my life to medicine, and that is no exaggeration. So, it is with awe, respect, and humility that we discuss how to improve medical research.

> *A world of analytical treasure awaits the analyst who crosses the barrier between text and a database.*

Existing medical records, at least the most important parts of the record, are in the form of text. It turns out that for analytical purposes, text has some systemic issues. The biggest difficulty of text (but hardly the only one) is that text must be read to be understood. And that requires a human to do the reading. The problem is that humans can only read and absorb a finite number of documents.

For all practical purposes, there are an infinite number of medical documents to read. We need a computer. The problem with having a computer handle a huge number of documents is that those documents cannot be in the form of text. Computers handle databases well. Computers do not handle text well at all.

And the volume of information is only the start of the problems with text. There are many other problems with text that we will discuss in this book.

For the most part, existing medical records are sparsely used or used cursory in existing medical research. If medical records are used in research at all, they are used in an almost sophomoric manner. We will cover how to use those records in a much more sophisticated and illuminating manner.

The nexus of this book is how to cross the barrier from text to a database for medical data.

In doing so, whole vistas of valuable information become available that were never available before. In the long run, this leads to better medicine, longer lives, and improved health.

To understand the profundity of this phenomenon, consider a simple analogy.

We are told that early man only had black, white, and grey vision. Then, the first man woke one day to find that he could see blues, reds, and greens. The blue of the sky. The red of the sunset. The green of the grass.

The man woke up and was excited. He rushed to his neighbor and started talking about beauty and color. And the neighbor (and everyone else in the world) did not know what the man was talking about. They thought the man was crazy. No one else had ever seen color before, and the descriptions offered sounded strange to someone who had never seen color.

Once researchers discover the value and secrets wrapped up in mountains of medical records, they can start to see things that they had never imagined. To unlock these secrets, it is necessary to cross the bridge between text and a database.

In this book, our example will use real medical records. These records do not violate the laws of HIPAA. The records we will use are from a country where HIPAA laws are not in force, collected before there was any HIPAA law, and have been de-identified.

We hope this book leads to healthier people and longer lives. That is our mission.

Bill Inmon
Denver, Colorado

Acknowledgments

The authors would like to acknowledge and thank the contributions of:

- Patty Haines
- Kathryn Shut
- John "Steggy" Stegeman
- Jamila Taylor

Patty, Kathryn, John, and Jamila built the analytics graphics in this book.

Chapter 1

The Need for Modernizing Medical Research of Medical Records

Medical records have been kept for a long time. These records are written by hand and reflect the journey of both doctors and patients as they have passed through the institution in the pursuit of better health. The medical records have documented the progression of diseases, medications, diagnoses, procedures, and treatments. The medical records have documented improved health and declining health. The medical records are a testament to the progress of medicine.

The study of the information found in medical records is extremely valuable to the practice of medicine.

Medical records chronicle the journey of the treatment, cure, and outcome in the eyes of the patient and the doctor. Medical records are a treasure trove of valuable information waiting to be analyzed.

Medical records memorialize:

- What treatments, medications, and procedures have worked
- What treatments, medications, and procedures have not worked
- What treatments, medications, and procedures are more effective than others
- What trends and patterns there are in the cure of a disease?
- What are typical symptoms?
- What are atypical symptoms?

And so forth.

With the information locked up in medical records, doctors can find the path to achieving more effective treatments. And that leads to the better health of everyone.

A treasure trove of information is locked up in medical records. However, unlocking that treasure trove is not a simple or easy thing to do.

Unlocking the treasure trove

The first step in unlocking the secrets of medical records is to examine the medical record itself. There are many different types of medical records, yet most medical records have a similar format.

> *A typical medical record has a prescribed section and a free form section.*

The prescribed section contains the patient name, the date of the episode of care, and other basic standard information.

The free form section of the medical record contains anything the doctor or nurse wants to write. This includes diagnostics, prescribed medications, procedures, remarkable patient vital signs, symptoms, and so forth. The doctor can create whatever observations they think might be relevant and useful.

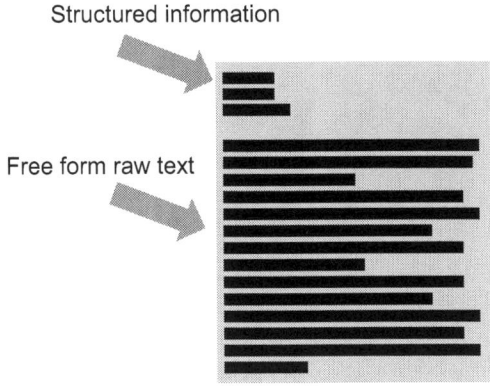

Figure 1: A typical medical record.

The most important section of the medical record is the free form component. The doctor writes down what is needed to know about the health and the care of the patient. At a later point in time, the doctor (or another doctor) can read the notes and continue caring for the patient.

Research and medical records

A doctor writes the medical record for the care and well-being of a single patient. That is the primary purpose of the medical record. A secondary purpose of the medical record is for research. Through research, the medical community starts to understand large medically related subjects such as the treatment of cancer, COVID, diabetes, and other afflictions.

Figure 2: Looking at a few records is not very helpful.

For the purpose of medical research, looking at only a handful of records is not effective. To understand broad topics of medicine, it is necessary to look at many patients, treatments, and outcomes. For this reason, research against medical records is done on as many relevant and accurate records as possible.

The primary value of analyzing medical records in research is understanding diseases and medical conditions affecting whole populations. The collective perspective gained by looking at a population is much valuable information. When you look at a population from a medical perspective, patterns and trends become apparent that would never be possible looking at a handful of records.

> *The insight that can be found by looking at whole populations is invaluable in learning how to treat a disease or a condition.*

The challenges of looking at a population

There are many reasons why looking at a population's medical records is a daunting task.

One challenge is that there are so many different kinds of medical records. Medical records can come from many different places where medicine is practiced: the operating room, pharmacy, laboratory, hospital, personal physician, and so forth. Each of these different sources of information has its own format, purpose, language, and so forth. The people who created one record have a different agenda than those who created another. Tying these records together is a challenge. Yet, to do analytics, this information must be connected.

Figure 3: There are different kinds of medical records.

A second challenge to looking at information across a population is that there are different vendors of medical record technology. The vendors have their own way of creating their medical records. There are different formats. There may be different terminology, and so forth. One vendor's practices in creating the medical record will be different from another vendor's practices. The fact that medical records can come from many places and many vendors complicates the life of the medical researcher. Connecting all this data in a cohesive and meaningful manner is challenging. But if there is to be a study of a population, this connection must be made.

Yet another complicating factor to creating a meaningful and cohesive body of knowledge from medical records across a population is that medical records exist on different storage media. Some records are on paper stuffed in files. Other records are on a computer. Other records are on voice recordings. Each of the different forms of media have their own considerations. To study medical records across a population, it is necessary to combine all the media on which medical records are stored.

Text as an obstacle

But the greatest obstacle to the effective study of medical records is that the most interesting and useful parts of the medical record are written in the form of text.

The fact that text is an obstacle is a surprise for many people. It doesn't appear on the surface to be an obstacle but text in fact is a great obstacle.

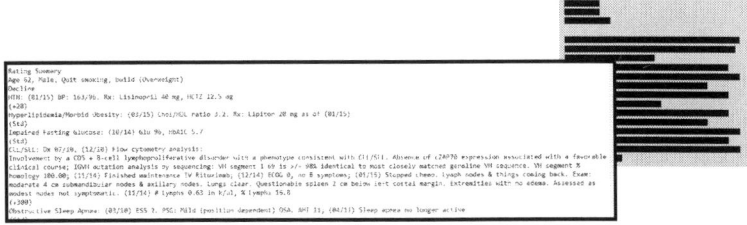

Figure 4: The important part of the medical record is in the form of text.

Text is an obstacle for a lot of reasons. Text is often imprecise. Text is sometimes not written properly. Text is full of ambiguities. Text may not be complete. Text can be easily understood. These are all impediments caused by the fact that medical records contain text. But the real reason why text is the obstacle that it is that text is read manually.

Because text has to be read manually means a human must read the text. And the problem with that is that a human can only read and comprehend so many documents. The human brain only has a limited capacity before it starts to overflow.

A computer must be used to handle a large (effectively unlimited) number of documents. There are a huge number of documents to be handled when it comes to medical records. Therefore, to do medical research on medical documents, a computer must be used.

> *A complication with using the computer is that the computer works well with databases and not much else.*

Databases contain neatly organized units of information that the computer can quickly access and analyze. The units of information in the database are uniform in terms of content. The computer finds, manipulates, and stores data quickly and efficiently when data is in the form of a database.

What a computer does not do well is to operate on text. Text is unstructured. Text is ambiguous. Text is free form and the computer struggles to make sense of text. Stated differently, the computer is optimized for operating on databases, not text. The computer views text as something that is essentially "messy". Unfortunately, the interesting part of medical records is in the form of text.

So there is a conundrum. Medical research requires that many records of data be accessed and analyzed. But those multitude of medical records are all wrapped up in the form of text.

A computer must be used to read and analyze a lot of medical records. And the computer demands that data be in the form of a database. But the records are in the form of text. That is the challenge facing the analyst wishing to unlock the secrets of the medical records. And it is a nontrivial challenge.

There is a significant and profound difference between text and a database. A database is well organized. Text is not organized at all. A database is highly structured. A medical record is unstructured. A database is optimized for access and analysis. A medical record is not optimized for access and analysis. And there are many other differences as well.

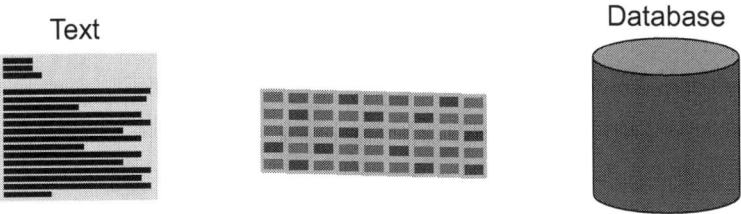

Figure 5: There is a complex and very real barrier between a database and textually based medical records.

Textual disambiguation

Fortunately, there is technology that bridges the gap between text and a database. That technology is textual Extract, Transform, and Load (ETL) or textual disambiguation. The really good news is that textual ETL is:

- Easy, simple to use
- Fast
- Economical
- Does not require consultants

A step by step approach

How can an organization go from raw medical records to a database? There is a simple, well-traveled path to be followed.

Step 1 is to gather medical records that need to be studied and processed. Step 2 is to pass the records through ingestion. Step 3 is to pass the text through textual ETL. Step 4 is to create and vet the database that has been produced out of textual ETL. Step 5 is to produce analytics from the database.

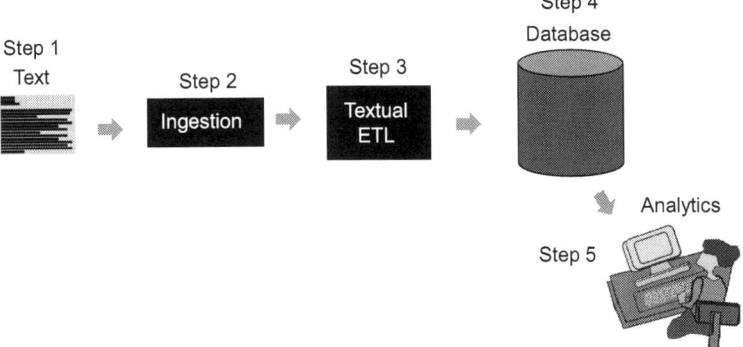

Figure 6: There is a five-step process needed to produce analytical results from raw text.

Each of these steps has many moving parts and challenges and will be discussed in detail in subsequent chapters.

From the standpoint of the decision maker, the most obvious and most important step is the production of the analytics that result from the creation of the database. The steps that lead up to the analysis are important to the production of the analysis. However, the payoff to the analyst is generated by the analysis.

Heuristic analysis

While the steps for doing analytics from medical records are straightforward as outlined, there is an overriding factor to consider. That factor is that research is normally done on the basis of exploring information. In other words, the research analyst merely starts by examining what is in a topic. After the analyst finds out what the components of a topic are, the analyst can now start to ask piercing questions based on the initial findings.

Most studies rarely have a single question being answered by the analysis. Instead, a panoply of information is laid bare, and the analyst picks out the most promising and interesting information that has been uncovered. The analysis continues looking for further elucidation of the interesting aspects of the topic being studied.

This method of analysis is called the heuristic approach to analysis. The heuristic analysis begins with some general questions and proceeds to more specific questions. Each level of analysis sets the stage for the next level of analysis. One level of discovery leads to another level of discovery, and so forth. The different levels of analysis only end when the analyst is satisfied.

From ah? to aha!

Because of the exploratory nature of the mindset of the analyst, the path through the analytical forest is never clear at the beginning. Furthermore, the path to the answer is not clear.

The heuristic nature of the analytical processing proceeds in an uncharted manner. There is no foreknowledge of:

- How long the analysis might take
- How many iterations of analysis there might be

- What the results of the analysis might be
- If there is even going to be a final result.

The heuristic path of analysis consists of repeating the same pattern of analysis. First, the text is prepared. This means that the text is transformed into a database. Analysis of the database ensues. From the analysis, insights are generated.

The insights that are generated then cause a rethinking of the text and the analysis. A new set of text is prepared and the database is analyzed. Insights are generated and the process is repeated.

It is noteworthy that each time a new analysis is generated, the data preparation is different. The first time a database is generated, the work done for the generation is substantial. But subsequent iterations usually only require a marginal amount of work to prepare the text.

This pattern of analytic processing is the norm for servicing the needs of the end user that wishes to do exploratory processing.

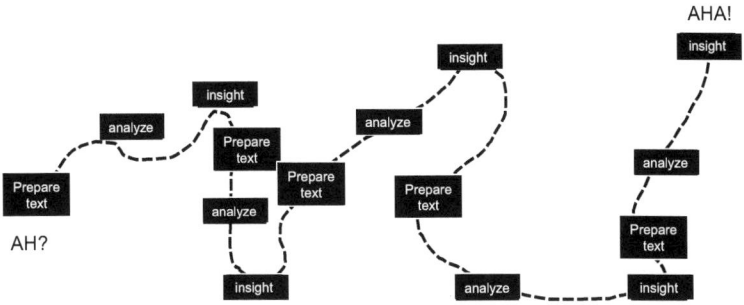

Figure 7: Heuristic processing from 'ah' to 'aha'.

The need for speed

Because of the discovery and exploratory nature of heuristic analysis, it is vitally important that the steps that have been described be done as quickly as possible. There is a real need for speed in creating the database and the ensuing analysis from the raw text. The reason for the need for speed is that the needs of the recipient of the information are sure to change as the analysis progresses. If the analysis is done slowly, the process of analysis loses momentum. In addition, in a fast-changing world, if an analysis takes too long, even the factors that shape the analysis can change.

> *The end user analyst operates in a mode of,*
> *"Give me what I say I want, then I can tell you*
> *what I really want."*

This mindset (which is very typical) mandates that there will be multiple iterations of analysis. The longer it takes to go through the different steps of each iteration that have been outlined, the less effective the study. To have an effective analysis, it is necessary to go through the different iterations of analysis as rapidly as possible.

So what changes can be made from one iteration of analysis to the next? The answer is that any aspect of the iterative process can change.

The end user analyst can:

- Decide to add new source material or modify existing raw text
- Decide to ingest the text differently
- Decide to change the way text is analyzed
- Decide to add or delete portions of the database
- Decide to analyze data differently

Or do all of the above.

In short, any aspect of the iterative analysis can be adjusted from one iteration to the next. The turnaround time between different iterations of analysis then is an important factor in research success. A turnaround time of one to two days is normally very effective. A turnaround time of a month is hardly optimal, and a turnaround time of a year is disastrous.

The more quickly an iteration of analysis can be done, the better.

The speed of iteration gives the analyst the freedom to ask "what if" questions. The more what-if questions that can be asked and answered, the more effective the analysis.

Obstacles to achieving speed of analysis

Many factors impede the progress of a research project:

- **Complexity of medical terms and practices.** Complexity introduces confusion and ambiguity. Confusion and ambiguity have a very deleterious effect on the success of an analysis. Trying to resolve confusion slows down the process of analysis.

- **Cost of iterating text.** If the cost of an analytical iteration is high, management may balk at funding doing iterations. And if management does not support the execution of iterations, the whole analysis is slowed.

- **Complexity of processing.** It is easy to get lost in the processing of text. And when researchers get lost, there is a delay in creating an iteration. There are many facets to text processing, and it is easy to lose the way to achieving the final result.

- **Completeness of data.** Rarely is data truly complete. There is always some more data to add. The analyst must determine when an adequate and relevant amount of data has been gathered.

- **Simplicity of processing.** The simpler the process is, the greater the chance that the process will be streamlined.

And there are other factors as well.

There is then a path that can be followed in order to start to unlock the treasures that are in medical records.

Autonomy of analysis

One of the key success factors that mitigates many of the obstacles to rapid iterative processing is the autonomy of the analyst in doing the different iterations that are processed. Things slow down when a third party starts to interject themselves into the analytical process. The third party has to learn about the business being analyzed, understand and prepare data and processing, and raise research expenses.

The more control the analyst has over the process of analysis, the better. Ceding control to a third party is poisonous.

If at all possible, the research analyst needs to be able to conduct the analysis without any interference or influence from a third party.

In summary

Medical records contain a treasure trove of valuable information. Medical records typically contain two parts – a structured part and a narrative part. The structured part of the medical record contains such things as date, patient id, vital signs and so forth. The textual part of the medical record contains a narrative of what the doctor wants to make note of. For the most part, the most useful part of a medical record the is textual part.

Medical records serve the needs of a single doctor and a single patient. But when looking at large populations of patients, the text portion of the medical record needs to be converted to a database. A computer and a database can be used to analyze thousands of patients all at once, something that cannot be done when the medical record is in the form of text.

As such, text becomes an obstacle to medical research that has to concern itself with whole populations of patients.

In order to do research on a large population, the text must be turned into a database. Once the text is turned into a database, an unlimited amount of data can be analyzed.

The benefit of being able to analyze thousands of patient records quickly and efficiently supports the exploration processing that the analyst needs to do. The fast turnaround of an analytical process allows the analyst the freedom to change the parameters of the analysis quickly.

There is then a real need for speed in the reading and analysis of thousands of medical records.

Chapter 2

Taxonomies and Ontologies

At the heart of the analysis of medical records is the need to convert the text found in medical records into a computerized database. A computerized database is mandatory simply because of the number of medical records that need to be studied. A human brain cannot start to keep track of the information wrapped up in the number of medical records that exist.

To convert a textual medical record into a database format, it is necessary to use some specialized technology. That specialized technology, textual ETL, reads the raw text found in the medical record and converts the medical record text to a database.

At the heart of the conversion process that occurs inside textual ETL is administrative data known as a taxonomy and/or an ontology.

Textual ETL reads raw text from the medical records and uses a taxonomy/ontology to produce a database record based on what has been read in the raw text of the medical record.

The medical research analyst needs to know what a taxonomy/ontology is and how the taxonomy/ontology influences the transformation of raw text from a medical record into a database format.

At the core of the intelligence of textual ETL is a taxonomy. The taxonomy helps us understand and interpret the raw text from the medical record passing through textual ETL. The raw text from the medical record that textual ETL is processing is passed through the elements of a taxonomy to determine if there is a match.

The analyst needs to understand a few rudiments of taxonomies and ontologies to understand textual ETL and how textual ETL can disambiguate text and build a database from the reading of raw text.

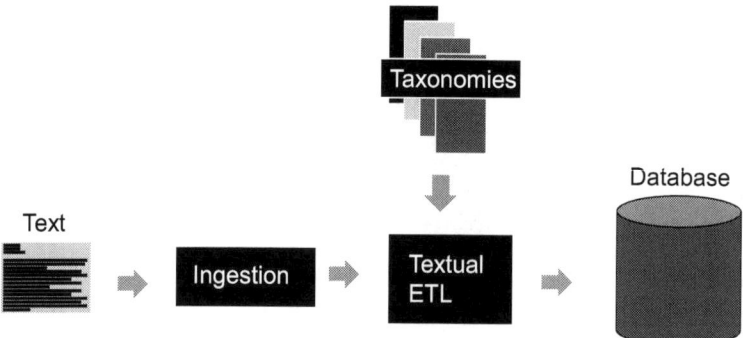

Figure 8: At the heart of textual ETL's ability to understand text are taxonomies.

Taxonomies

In many ways, the taxonomies which textual ETL uses are the "brains" of textual disambiguation. Taxonomies are used to recognize what is going on with the text that textual ETL is processing. Taxonomies are used to separate extraneous words found in raw text from the words needed for analytical processing.

A taxonomy is nothing more than a classification of some words that are of interest. For example, a taxonomy might be a tree type. Different types of trees belong to the tree type, such as elm, oak, pine, and sycamore. Or a taxonomy might be for types of cars. This taxonomy might include Porsche, Ford, Toyota, and Honda.

Given that a taxonomy can be used for any kind of classification, there is an effectively unlimited number of taxonomies. There are taxonomies for trees. For car types. For States. For musical instruments. The only limitation to the types of classification of words that can reside inside a taxonomy is the imagination of the analyst.

Figure 9: A taxonomy is a classification. It can be of anything.

Relevance

The usefulness of a taxonomy in interpreting raw text is a relative matter. For a taxonomy to be useful, the elements of the taxonomy have to be relevant to the text being analyzed. For example, a taxonomy for disease and medication is useful for analyzing medical data. But a taxonomy of car parts and rock and roll music would be unlikely to be useful in analyzing medical data.

To better understand what a taxonomy is, consider what a taxonomy is not. As an example of what isn't a taxonomy, consider the list of words shown in Figure 10. In the example, the list is supposedly about trees. But in the list is found baseball, the Navajo tribe, and a Porsche, which are decidedly not trees.

Figure 10: Not a taxonomy.

The words found in a taxonomy must all be of the same classification type. Otherwise, the list of words is just a list, not a taxonomy.

Completeness of the taxonomy

An interesting property of taxonomies is that taxonomies are seldom complete, or at least as complete as they can be. Instead, taxonomies are complete insofar as the words contained therein are adequate to select words from raw text. There almost always are words that fit a taxonomy's classification but are not included in the taxonomy because they are not relevant to the text being analyzed. As a simple example of including only the right words, consider raw text that is being analyzed that relates to North American trees. The taxonomy for trees would include North American trees such as oak, elm, and pecan. But the taxonomy would not include baobab, eucalyptus, and the Amarula tree. The disincluded trees are native to other countries.

Unique identification

The classification of words found in a taxonomy does not imply that each unit of text that has been classified can be uniquely identified. A word coming from raw text may be classified but not uniquely identified. To illustrate that individual items are not uniquely identified, consider a taxonomy for a forest. The taxonomy for the forest will classify the different kinds of trees found in the forest. But the taxonomy for the forest will not give a unique identifier to each tree. When the word "pine" is encountered in raw text, the taxonomy will classify "pine" as a tree, but will not specify a particular pine tree.

Medical taxonomies

The taxonomies used by textual ETL to sort through raw text are relevant to the subject of the raw text. For example, when looking at medically related data, the types of taxonomies that might be included are:

- Medications
- Procedures
- Diseases
- Hospitals
- Symptoms
- Outcomes
- Diagnoses

But when analyzing medical texts, you would not expect to find taxonomies on fishing, gold mining, and water skiing.

Depending on the particulars of the raw text being analyzed, there may well be other taxonomies that will need to be added.

In addition, if the raw text being analyzed is highly specialized, adding words to an already existing taxonomy may be necessary. Fortunately, it is very easy to add new words and classify them when needed.

As an example, suppose text about kidney patients is being analyzed. It may be necessary to add mycophenolate to the medication list if mycophenolate is not already there. Fortunately, it is easy to adjust the contents of a taxonomy if needed.

TAXONOMIES AND ONTOLOGIES • 31

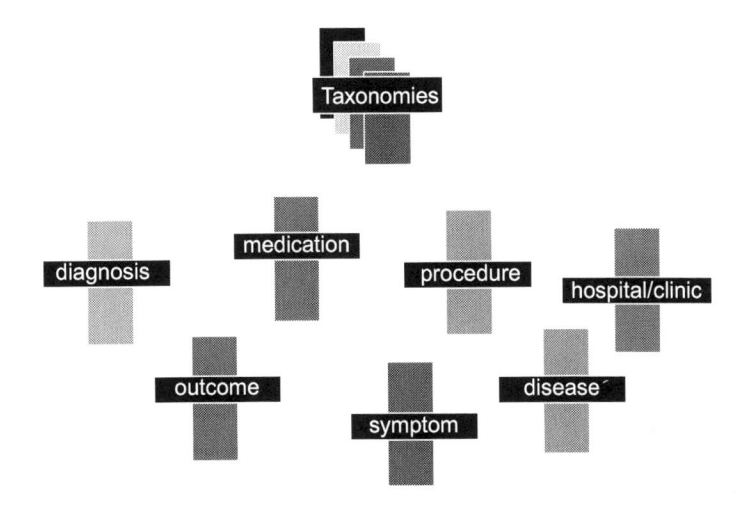

Figure 11: Some typical taxonomies that might be used in the disambiguation of medical data.

How are taxonomies used?

What then is the role that a taxonomy plays in the interpretation of raw text? Exactly how is the taxonomy used to unlock valuable data from raw text? The taxonomies used by textual ETL accomplish the following:

- Inclusion in the taxonomy indicates that a word that has been found in the raw text that needs to be included in the database that is being formed.

- Once a word has been found in raw text, the context of the word is derived from the taxonomy.

- The occurrence of words found together further indicates a relationship of data among the words.

These three elements of the raw text form the basis of the creation of the database that is useful for analytical processing. So exactly what are the dynamics of a taxonomy and raw text in the capture and interpretation of raw text as the raw text moves through textual ETL?

Consider the following example:

There are three taxonomies: a surgery taxonomy, a provider taxonomy, and a medication taxonomy. There is a simple sentence made up of raw text about a patient's journey through medical treatment. As the raw text is read, each word is compared to the words found in the taxonomies. A hit occurs on the words ablation, doctor, and lisinopril. The ablation procedure is determined to be a form of surgery. The doctor is a healthcare provider. The drug lisinopril is determined to be a medication.

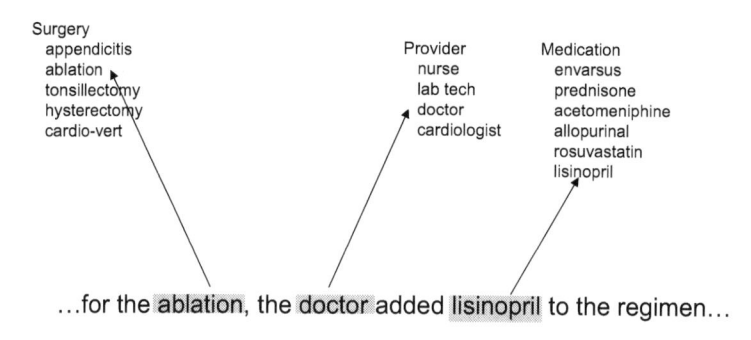

```
Surgery
    appendicitis
    ablation
    tonsillectomy
    hysterectomy
    cardio-vert

Provider
    nurse
    lab tech
    doctor
    cardiologist

Medication
    envarsus
    prednisone
    acetomeniphine
    allopurinal
    rosuvastatin
    lisinopril
```

...for the ablation, the doctor added lisinopril to the regimen...

Figure 12: The raw text is read and matches to the taxonomies are identified.

Once found in both the raw text and the taxonomy, these words are placed in the database that will be used for further analysis, along with the context of the words.

A real world, external foundation

It is worthy of note that the taxonomies are formed by conformance to the real world, not by the text that is being analyzed. If the raw text were used to select words for inclusion into the taxonomies, the taxonomy would be limited to the scope of words found in the raw text. This would limit the scope to which the taxonomy would be used. Instead, the scope of the words found in the taxonomy is derived from the world external to the raw text. This enlargement of the scope of words greatly expands the usage of the taxonomy to many different forms of raw text.

As a simple example, suppose the text to be analyzed is about the rear suspension of a Porsche. The taxonomy would be based on the rear suspension of all commonly made cars, not just Porsches. In doing so, the taxonomy could be used to analyze text about many cars, not just Porsches.

The size of the taxonomy

Sometimes a taxonomy grows too large. All sorts of problems arise when a taxonomy exceeds the useful parameters of its existence. Processing times slow down to a crawl. All sorts of overlap and ambiguities start to occur. The costs of processing and storage start to expand. The taxonomy should encompass only the likely range of the text that is likely to be encountered. Furthermore, the taxonomy should be focused. If the taxonomy is aimed at trees in North America, it should not contain trees found only in Asia.

Periodic maintenance

However the taxonomy is built, it must be recognized that taxonomies require periodic maintenance. The good news is that normal maintenance is only done infrequently and for small numbers of words. Language changes, but at a slow pace and across a few words.

Ontologies

Another related structure found in processing textual ETL is that of an ontology. An ontology is nothing more than a collection of taxonomies. The ontology is the vessel that holds the different taxonomies used by textual ETL to interpret raw text. The taxonomies that are entered into the ontology may or may not have an interrelationship of the elements found in the taxonomies. Figure 13 shows that the ontology is for geography.

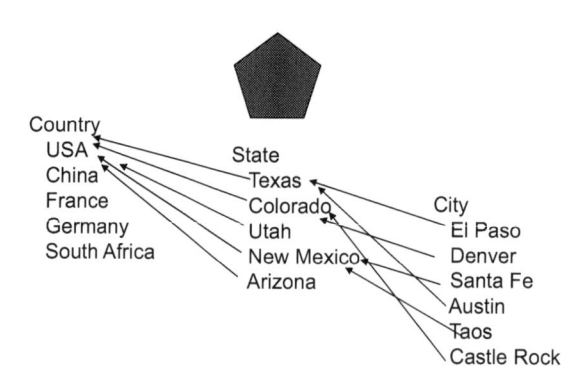

Figure 13: An ontology for geography. Taxonomies can be grouped together to form an ontology.

There are three taxonomies in the geography ontology: country, state, and city. Certain elements in one taxonomy may relate to other elements in another taxonomy within the same ontology.

On the other hand, there may not be a direct relationship among the elements in a taxonomy that are found in an ontology, and that is perfectly normal and acceptable. The following figure shows that there is an ontology about gourmet dining. There is no known direct relationship between the various elements found in the taxonomies that comprise the ontology.

Meat
  hamburger
  t bone steak
  porterhouse steak
  filet mignon
  chateaubriand

Wine
  Paul Masson
  Chateau Lafitte
  Chateau Margaux
  Gallo
  Maneschewitz

Chef
  Wolfgang Puck
  Julia Child
  Gordon Ramsey
  Bobbie Flay
  Anthony Bourdain

Figure 14: The gourmet ontology. The taxonomies inside an ontology do not have to be related.

In summary

To make the transformation from text to database, it is necessary to read text and use taxonomies to transform the text into a database. As such, the taxonomy becomes the "brains" of the transformation process. A taxonomy is nothing more than a classification of words. Every word in the taxonomy has the same relationship to the taxonomy as every other word. Taxonomies can be combined together to form larger taxonomies. And different taxonomies can be combined to form an ontology. An ontology is a grouping of different taxonomies that form a definition for some large subject area.

There is an unlimited number of data classifications. The taxonomies that populate an ontology all relate to the general subject area of the ontology. All of the taxonomies in an ontology are relevant to the subject area of the ontology.

Taxonomies are rarely complete. The taxonomies contain the words that are relevant to the subject area of the ontology. Taxonomies are used for the classifications of words, not the unique identification of words. Typical medical taxonomies include medication, procedure, disease, general terms of medicine, specific terms for medical specialties, and medical acronyms, among other subjects. Taxonomies are used when text is read and the raw text is compared to the elements in the taxonomy. Taxonomies are created from an external view of medicine, not the contents of the documents being studied.

On occasion, the size of a taxonomy grows to be so large that it needs to be trimmed to reduce its size. Such a trimming is a practical consideration of the usage of the taxonomy. Periodic maintenance must be done to the taxonomy. In addition, taxonomies can be customized to prepare them for use in a particular study.

Chapter 3

Ingesting Text

Text relevant to the medical researcher exists in many forms and many places. Much text is potentially useful to the medical researcher. However, to be used analytically, text must be converted from where it originally existed into an electronic format acceptable for analytical processing. In some cases, converting text into an acceptable electronic format is trivial. In other cases, the conversion is not trivial at all. Medical records need to be converted into a format acceptable for processing before any analysis can occur.

Privacy and the law

One overriding consideration of managing text for medical research is that medical text is subject to the laws of privacy and security that rule the country where the medical records reside.

There should be no need or desire to operate outside the boundaries of those laws. In the United States, the laws governing medical data use are called HIPAA. Other countries have their own laws governing medical information.

The primary focus of the laws governing medical documents is the protection of the privacy of the patient. As long as medical data is deidentified, the medical records are safe for processing and transport. Conversely, when medical records are not deidentified, they are not safe for analytical processing.

A simple form of deidentification appears in Figure 15. The patient's name is masked to protect the medical data in the example shown. But the remainder of the data remains untouched by the deidentification process.

The patient Bill Inmon had a kidney transplant on Nov 29, 2023 at Porter....

⬇

The patient xxxxxxxx had a kidney transplant on Nov 29, 2023 at Porter.....

Figure 15: HIPAA – deidentification of data.

Deidentification entails more than just name information. Deidentification involves any personally identifying information, such as Social Security number. In addition, deidentification can involve more detailed identifying secondary information, such as age, race, and gender.

Storage media

Medical records can reside on a variety of storage media. Typical storage media include:

- Paper-based records
- Voice-based records
- Electronic-based records

The analyst analyzing medical records needs to be aware of the considerations of each media style.

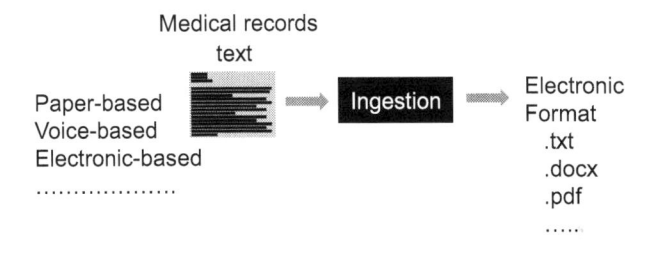

Figure 16: The goal is to transform the medical data into an electronically acceptable form.

Images

Can images be processed as well as text? For example, can a person analyze x-ray records? The answer is yes, the text on an x-ray record can be lifted and analyzed. But the actual image itself cannot be analyzed using the techniques that are described. This is true for all kinds of images, not just x-rays.

The same considerations are true for numeric data. The purpose of the analysis that is being described applies only to text, not raw numbers or images. In addition, handwritten text, cursive, cannot be processed in an automatic manner. For text to be processed, it must be cast in a standard font.

Medical record selection

One of the significant issues in successfully analyzing the text of medical records is the selection of the documents to be analyzed. This consideration is of particular interest to the analyst conducting the study of medical records.

In almost every case, the analyst wishes to have parameters guiding the selection of medical records to include in the analysis. Documents are chosen in accordance with the nature and goals of the study.

For example, a study on gynecology would probably not want to include men.

Typical selection criteria might be:

- Sex – men
- Age – 25 – 65
- Race – any
- Weight – 190 and above
- Education – some college

These analytical parameters guide the scope of the study and are used to select which medical records for inclusion in the study.

On occasion, the analyst wants to build a general-purpose database that will suit many different kinds of analysis. In this case, any and all medical records are selected for the database. Selection criteria are included on each record so that future analysts have quick access to the data found in the medical record.

> *Whether the data is being constructed for a particular study or whether the data is being constructed for general future usage, the selection criteria need to be considered at the onset of ingesting medical record data.*

Medical record structure

To consider the ingestion of a medical record, it is necessary to look at the typical structure of a medical record. Figure 17 illustrates what a typical medical record structure looks like.

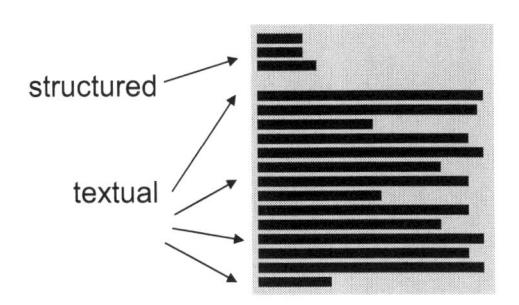

Figure 17: The structure of a medical record.

The medical record structure has two distinct parts: the structured part of the record and the textual (or free-form) portion of the medical record.

The structured part of the medical record typically has identifying information for the patient and the doctor. In addition, typically there is date information, location information, and other miscellaneous information that is useful for locating and describing the contents of the record. The structured information varies widely from one medical record vendor to another and across the boundaries of medical practice. For example, surgery may have a different structured component of its medical records than emergency medicine.

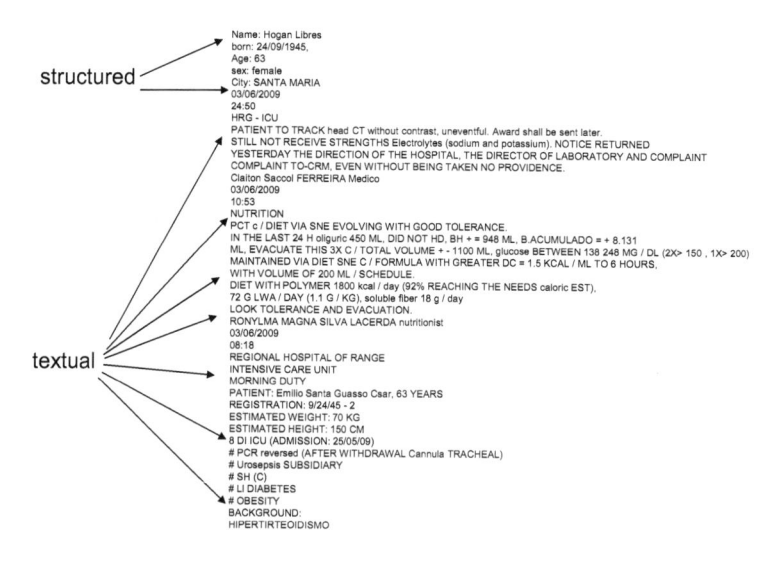

```
                    Name: Hogan Libres
                    born: 24/09/1945,
                    Age: 63
   structured       sex: female
                    City: SANTA MARIA
                    03/06/2009
                    24:50
                    HRG - ICU
                    PATIENT TO TRACK head CT without contrast, uneventful. Award shall be sent later.
                    STILL NOT RECEIVE STRENGTHS Electrolytes (sodium and potassium). NOTICE RETURNED
                    YESTERDAY THE DIRECTION OF THE HOSPITAL, THE DIRECTOR OF LABORATORY AND COMPLAINT
                    COMPLAINT TO-CRM, EVEN WITHOUT BEING TAKEN NO PROVIDENCE.
                    Claiton Saccol FERREIRA Medico
                    03/06/2009
                    10:53
                    NUTRITION
                    PCT c / DIET VIA SNE EVOLVING WITH GOOD TOLERANCE.
                    IN THE LAST 24 H oliguric 450 ML, DID NOT HD, BH + = 948 ML, B.ACUMULADO = + 8.131
                    ML, EVACUATE THIS 3X C / TOTAL VOLUME + - 1100 ML, glucose BETWEEN 138 248 MG / DL (2X> 150 , 1X> 200)
                    MAINTAINED VIA DIET SNE C / FORMULA WITH GREATER DC = 1.5 KCAL / ML TO 6 HOURS,
                    WITH VOLUME OF 200 ML / SCHEDULE.
                    DIET WITH POLYMER 1800 kcal / day (92% REACHING THE NEEDS caloric EST),
                    72 G LWA / DAY (1.1 G / KG), soluble fiber 18 g / day
                    LOOK TOLERANCE AND EVACUATION.
                    RONYLMA MAGNA SILVA LACERDA nutritionist
                    03/06/2009
                    08:18
     textual        REGIONAL HOSPITAL OF RANGE
                    INTENSIVE CARE UNIT
                    MORNING DUTY
                    PATIENT: Emilio Santa Guasso Csar, 63 YEARS
                    REGISTRATION: 9/24/45 - 2
                    ESTIMATED WEIGHT: 70 KG
                    ESTIMATED HEIGHT: 150 CM
                    8 DI ICU (ADMISSION: 25/05/09)
                    # PCR reversed (AFTER WITHDRAWAL Cannula TRACHEAL)
                    # Urosepsis SUBSIDIARY
                    # SH (C)
                    # LI DIABETES
                    # OBESITY
                    BACKGROUND:
                    HIPERTIRTEOIDISMO
```

Figure 18: While both the structured and textual components of the medical record are important, the most interesting part of the medical record is the textual component. Furthermore, in terms of size, the textual component of a medical record is the largest.

A complexity that some researchers face when looking across a body of medical records is the issue of the records residing in multiple languages. Most medical records, but not all, are found in English. This presents a challenge to the researcher. To do serious analysis against the medical records, the text needs to be in one language.

Should it arise, there are two ways to handle the issue of multiple languages for medical records.

It is assumed that there is some base language in which the analysis will be done. All medical records must be converted to this language if they are written natively in that language.

The first way to process multiple-language medical records is to read the records in their native language and use textual ETL to process the records. Textual ETL can handle different commonly used languages. This works well if the language in which the medical records are written is supported by textual ETL. Then, after the records are processed in their native language, the results are translated into the base language selected for the analysis.

For example, suppose there are records in German that need to be analyzed, and the base language is English. The medical records pass through textual ETL in German. The results are then translated into English and combined with the other medical records in the study. The alternative is to translate the records into the base language before they are processed, then process the records and place the results in the base language.

For example, suppose the records are in Dutch and the base language is English. The records are translated into English before they are processed. Then, the records are passed through textual ETL, and the results are combined with other data from the study.

Managing volumes of data

Another issue arising from ingesting medical records is the volume of the medical records to process. In some cases, only a handful of medical records need to be processed. In other cases, there are a very large number of medical records to be processed.

If there is a very large number of medical records to be processed, an easy alternative is to divide the records into separate collections and process the collections of records on separate machines. This is called parallel processing. You can process on as many different machines at the same time as you desire. The ability to process records in parallel means that there is no upper limit on how many records can be processed and how fast those records can be processed.

After the medical records are processed on different machines, the results are combined into one database, which becomes the basis for analysis. There is no technological reason why you can't do parallel processing. But there is an economic consideration. There is a cost associated with adding a new machine.

An alternative approach is to process the medical records over a period of time. The medical records processed in April can be added to the medical records processed in May with no problem.

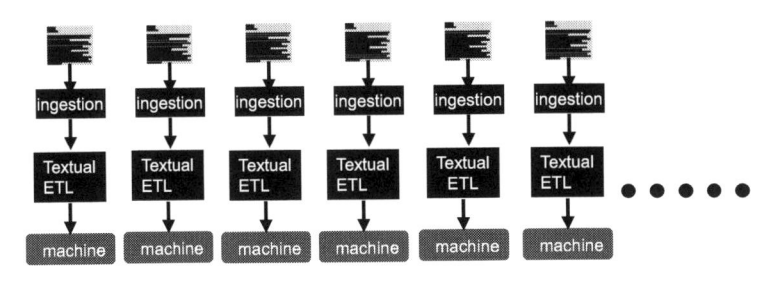

Figure 19: For large workloads, parallelism is built into textual ETL. Any workload can be handled.

Different data formats

In addition to medical records being stored on multiple media, medical records are stored in different formats. Each storage format has its own unique requirements and considerations. The research analyst needs to be apprised of what each of those requirements are. The typical formats in which medical records are stored include:

- Email
- Voice
- Spreadsheets
- Print
- Internet
- Database

Figure 20 depicts these formats.

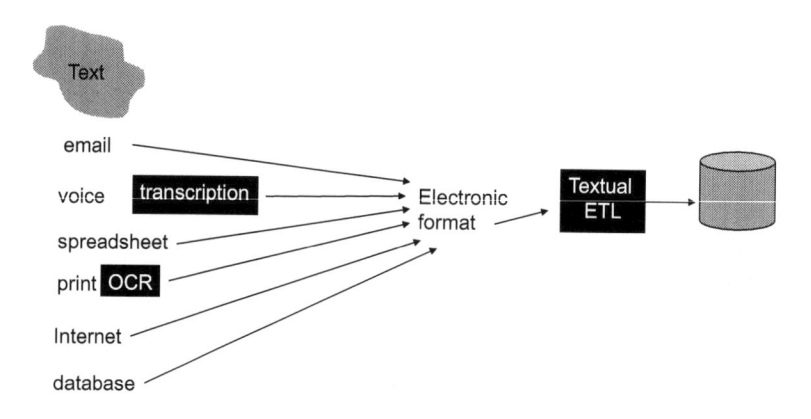

Figure 20: The first challenge is the access of text. The access of text is nontrivial.

Medical records stored in a database format have the property of being very diverse in content, very undisciplined. In addition, when accessing medical records in a database, a custom interface to the database needs to be written for each source of data.

Usually, this custom interface is simple. Nevertheless, the custom interface must be written.

The Internet

Occasionally, relevant and useful medical information is found on the Internet. The good news is that the text found on the Internet is already in an electronic format. The second piece of good news is that if medical information is found on the Internet, there are few security considerations.

The bad news is that some sites do not want large amounts of data or text to be lifted from the Internet. These sites go out of their way to prevent mass access. The second piece of bad news is that the interface to each site is unique. This means customized software must be written to access the site.

Furthermore, the site interfaces change frequently. This means that constant updates to the site interfaces must be done frequently.

In print

Many medical records are found in print. For years before there was the computer, medical records were stored in print in folders stuffed into a library. Older institutions have a whole room or two full of these older files.

While older information may not be relevant to an existing patient, valuable information may still be hidden in those records. There is technology called OCR (optical character recognition) that lifts the text off the page and into an electronic medium in an electrical format. OCR technology has been around for a long time and is quite mature. There are, however, some considerations to using OCR.

One consideration is that OCR nearly always demands some manual effort to operate. Someone has to find the printed file, remove it from its shelf, and load it into the OCR capture device. This simple act must be repeated over and over. The task itself is not difficult. But the number of times it has to be repeated is daunting. A second challenge of using OCR is that, on occasion, the transformation from paper to electronics is not done correctly. The result is erroneous data in an electronic format.

There are several factors that shape the quality of the transformation. Those factors are:

- **Font**. If the original document was written in a non-standard font, the transformation may be faulty.

- **Ink strike**. If the printed document was written at the end of the life of the ribbon, the ink strike would often be faint. When the ink strike is faint, the reader has a hard time depicting the original text.

- **Paper quality**. On occasion, the paper on which the document is written is so old or inferior that the process of reading the document does not work well.

The problem is that when the text arrives in an electronic format and the text is not accurate, the integrity of the analysis comes into question.

Spreadsheets

Another location where medical records sometimes hide is that of spreadsheets. Spreadsheets are available to anyone who has a personal computer. They are ubiquitous and easily available.

But there are some problems with spreadsheets. The first problem with spreadsheets is that the integrity of the text found on spreadsheets is always questionable. Anyone can write anything on a spreadsheet. As such, the analyst must always question the validity of the text derived from a spreadsheet. A second problem with a spreadsheet is that numeric values cannot be reliably lifted because the meaning and context of the numbers must be determined first.

On a voice recording

When medical records are stored on a recording in the format of a voice, they, too, can be entered into textual ETL. Voice records require the same transcription technology as records stored in print. Instead of OCR, voice transformation requires what is called voice transcription technology. Voice transcription technology listens to the recording of a voice and converts what is being said into an electronic format.

Of course, voice transcription can be done manually. But manual voice transcription is very expensive to do.

Automated voice transcription works well, except that voice transcription is never 100% accurate. Inevitably, some words are misunderstood during the transcription process. How many words are misunderstood? The transcription will probably be useful if the percentage of correct interpretations is high. But if the percentage of errors is high, the transcription may not be worth using.

There are many factors which influence the quality of the voice transcription of medical records, including:

- The quality of the equipment used to do the recording
- The quality of the line transmission
- The tone of the speaker (some people speak very softly)
- The accent of the speaker.

Email

Email can be a source of text useful to the medical researcher. There are, however, some considerations of using email. The first concern in using email is that in a typical email stream, many emails are irrelevant to the researcher. These emails need to be removed because they "clutter up" the data that is produced. If the emails that are not useful come from outside the organization, they are called "spam". If the unuseful emails come from inside the organization, they are called "blather". A second issue with using emails for medical research is that emails carry a large amount of administrative overhead, which is useful only to the system managing the email. The analyst is only interested in the text of the email, not the administrative system overhead that comes with the email. If the administrative overhead of the email is not removed, the analyst's life will be much more difficult. This overhead needs to be removed before the email can be processed.

In summary

A consideration when reading and using medical records is conformance to privacy laws. In the United States, there are HIPAA laws that require adherence. Other countries have their own privacy considerations.

When medical records need privacy protection, the records can be deidentified. Deidentification requires that information such as Social Security number and name be protected.

The first step in processing text into a usable electronic format is the ingestion of the text. Text to ingest can reside on several different media, with each of the media on which text resides having its own idiosyncrasies and considerations.

One of the considerations for an analysis is the selection criteria for which medical records will be included in a study and which will not be selected. Typical selection criteria include age, gender, weight, ethnicity, past medical history, and so forth.

In addition to the storage media having its criteria for usage, the format of the data has its own set of considerations. The different storage formats include email, spreadsheets, the Internet, print, voice, and database. Each of the formats of data has its own considerations.

The net result of ingestion is converting raw text into an acceptable electronic format.

Chapter 4

Research Journals and Clinical Trials

Textual ETL is good for medical research for doctors who want to look at the text locked up in medical records. And there is plenty of information locked up in those medical records. There is, however, another interesting place to look for medical information. That place is in medical journals.

Medical journals

There are actually a lot of medical journals. And these medical journals present to the public the latest in medical research. As such, there is valuable information there. All of the information found in those journals is presented in the form of text and diagrams.

There is then, a reliable and valuable source of important medical information tied up in the form of text that lies in other than a doctor's medical records.

Clinical trials and patient records

However, there is an important difference between the information found in medical journals and patient records. Research journals document the results of carefully controlled and measured tests. As such, they are bellwethers of the future and what can be done in terms of better medicine. On the other hand, patient records are a memorialization of the past. Patient records define what past activities and past outcomes have been. Patient records are not created in a controlled environment. Instead, patient records simply describe the journey of a patient as best the doctor sees it.

The difference between research data and medical records does not negate or in any way diminish the value of the information found there. However, there must be a constant awareness of this fundamental difference.

Both types of medical information can yield important information that can lead to the advancement of medicine. Both forms of information are potentially valuable to the better practice of medicine.

Another difference is that clinical trials restrict themselves to a limited body of carefully selected patients. Medical records do not have that restriction. Medical records can be examined over a huge body of patients.

Text and clinical trials

Research journals and clinical trials are made up, for the most part, of text. There might be charts and illustrations, but most is in the form of text. There can be great value in committing these research-based documents to a database, in the same manner as medical records can be committed to a database. Once committed to a database, analysis can be done over unlimited research papers and clinical trials.

One of the positive aspects of using published research documents as a basis for a database is that the text found in research papers is not terribly difficult to ingest, unlike medical records, which indeed can be very difficult to ingest.

There is one issue that the analyst building the textually based database must be aware of. Not all authors and owners of intellectual property disclosed about a clinical study desire to have their findings converted to a database. Therefore, before placing text from a clinical study into a database, the analyst needs to be sure that it is legal to do so.

Aside from the systemic perspective of the differences between medical records and medical research on clinical trials, there are some other differences between the types of medical information that are of note:

- **Funding**. Medical research and clinical trials are often sponsored by external organizations, such as pharmaceuticals and medical suppliers. Medical records from a doctor are not sponsored by a large organization.

- **Conflict of interest**. There may well be a conflict of interest in the providers of medical research for the clinical trial and the researchers who have conducted the study. Medical doctors, on the other hand, do not have conflicts of interest in the treatment of a patient.

- **Size**. Medical research and clinical trials are applied to a small, controlled group of patients and subjects. Medical records written by a doctor are for whole entire populations and are not tightly controlled.

- **Protocol**. There is a protocol for disclosing information gathered while doing research for a clinical trial. There is a different protocol for disclosing information gathered by a doctor treating a patient.

- **History**. Rarely is medical research predicated on historical observations. Of course, previous medical research and practices set the stage for a clinical trial. But the trial itself is forward-looking, not backward-looking. Medical research creates its own carefully controlled, limited history of observations. The conclusions made from medical records are based on historical observations.

- **Quantity**. Research and clinical trials are based on a finite number of highly controlled observations. Conclusions drawn for looking at medical records are based on a very large number of uncontrolled observations.

These differences between research and medical records are just the tip of the iceberg.

Having stated that, the improvement of medicine using text analytics can be based on both types of data.

The structure of the study

The structure of a typical research paper is quite different from the structure of a medical record. Having stated that, there really is no standard format for creating a medical research document.

There is, however, a lot of similarity and uniformity in the format of research documents. The typical structure of a research document is:

- **Title.** A terse description of the contents of the document.

- **Abstract.** A short narrative describing the basic contents of the document.

- **Summary.** A narrative of the findings.

- **Conflict of interest statement.** A disclosure of any potential conflicts of interest by the authors.

- **Authors.** An identification of the principals conducting the study.

- **Key words.** Important words used for searching that are found in the study.

- **Introduction.** A statement of what is being studied.

- **Description.** A narrative of the study, usually a long discourse describing all the elements of the study.

- **Results.** The findings of the study.

- **Acknowledgments.** A mention of contributors.

- **Supplemental.** A location of related material.

- **Reviewers.** External parties that have reviewed the study.

Not all studies have all of these sections of text. In some cases, a section of text may simply not be applicable.

The number of studies/clinical trials

Many medical journals produce the findings of many different studies. Furthermore, different and varying clinical trials are constantly forthcoming. Because of the number of studies and the rate at which they are produced, it is difficult to stay abreast of medical advances.

However, by moving the results and contents of the many clinical trial studies to a database, it is much easier to stay in touch with the advancements being made in medicine. Once the text found in the studies is in the form of a database, the computer can easily handle the volume of studies.

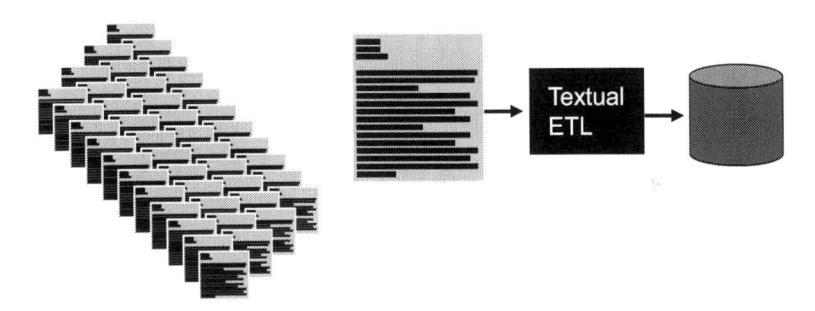

Figure 21: By moving the contents of a research project to a database, it is possible to keep up with medical research.

For many reasons, analyzing a database and using the database for analysis is far easier to do when there are a lot of records and new records are being created at warp speed.

Reading the entire document

One of the interesting benefits of committing research text about clinical trials to a database is that the analyst can go into the entire document by using new technology to manage text in a database. In an earlier day and age, the analyst only looked at the abstract because looking at an abstract was an efficient thing to do. However, with a computer approach to reading and managing text, the analyst can go into the entire research report. In doing so, much information is discovered by reading the entire report that would previously have been overlooked.

When the analyst tries to scan existing research material, most analysts just look at the abstract of a research paper. While the abstract contains important information, the body of the document contains more detailed information. When using a computer to read the document, there is no reason why the entire research document should not be read and committed to a database. In doing so, important details are recorded that otherwise would have been overlooked.

Creating a database in an automated manner mitigates the practice of just looking at the abstract of the document.

Resolving terminology differences

Another major benefit of committing research text to a database is that when looking at and comparing information across multiple research documents, it is easy to resolve terminology differences across the documents. One document refers to the cranium. Another document refers to the skull.

While a person reading the two documents will make the connection, the computer won't make the connection unless told to do so.

With textual ETL, it is easy to make connections between documents even when different terminology is used in different research studies.

The technology which automates the transformation of text into a database makes the analysis of studies whose text has been committed to a database easy and natural.

The large number of research documents in journals that are created guarantees that there will be differences in terminology that need to be resolved. Stated differently, the volume of research documents that are encountered exaggerates the issue of the need for terminology resolution.

In summary

While doctors' notes are a rich source of information, research papers about clinical trials are another source of valuable medical information.

There are two fundamental differences between doctors' notes and clinical trials. Doctors' notes merely state the doctors' observations over a large population. Research studies operate on a carefully selected and controlled group of patients. Doctors' notes reflect the past history of a patient. Clinical trials project the future by observing patients in a controlled trial.

Chapter 5

Unification of Text

Certainly, the work of ingesting text from various medical sources is its own challenge. But merely ingesting text is only the first step in building a foundation for doing analytics on medical text. The next step in building the foundation is the unification of the text and the data that has been ingested.

Unification of text refers to the transformation of the many sources of text into a singular form that can be analyzed.

Why does text coming from many sources need to be unified? Consider the following simple example. There are two medical records that need to be placed into a database: record A and record B.

These records look like:

	Record A	Record B
Gender	male	X
Medication	furosemide	Lasix
Weight	175 pounds	76 kilograms
Hospital	Guadalupe de Hidalgo	St Mary's

These records have a lot of common information, but the information is not expressed in a consistent manner. If these records were placed in a database, the database analyst would have to convert all of these values into a common format before any analysis could begin. The format and contents of the records themselves become a large barrier to success. Now consider what would happen if the analyst had 100,000 records to process. The analyst would have to convert 100,000 records into a common format before analysis could begin. The analyst would spend all of his/her time doing data conversions and not doing analysis.

To do the analysis properly, the analyst needs to convert record values into a common format before placing the medical records into a database, not after the records have been placed into a database. For this reason, the architect building the infrastructure for the research of medical records must sequence the conversion properly.

There are many sources of medical records and medical research that have many different ways of recording a patient's journey. Furthermore, when the text for the medical record or the research journal was originally written or otherwise communicated, no author coordinated with any other author to unify what was communicated.

The result is that collecting lots of text from random sources is very scattered. Each author has their own way of organizing and describing their observations.

To do analytics efficiently, the text and the data that is generated by the text must be unified across all sources. Unification of text and data is a large and complex topic, yet the unification of text and data must be done before analyzing that text and data.

To understand the need for unification of text and data, consider a simple example. Suppose that there are many sources of medical text that need to be placed into a database, and suppose that the sources of information come in different languages. The sources are read and ingested. However, once they are ingested, they need to be placed into the database that is created for analysis. Do they need to be translated before they are placed into the database? If they are not translated before they are placed into the database, the analyst who tries to use the database will have to do the translation before doing any analysis. To be useful for analysis, there must be a single language in which the text and data are stored.

The inevitable conclusion is that the translation from the many source documents needs to be done before the text and data are placed into the database.

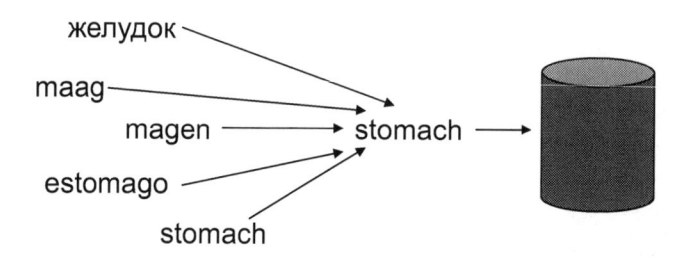

Figure 22: Data needs to be unified before being placed in the database.

The good news is that there is technology that supports the unification of text and data before the text and data are placed into the analytical database. That technology is textual ETL or textual disambiguation.

So exactly what does the unification of text and data mean? The answer is that it means many things. It has many facets.

Encoding

Encoding of data refers to how data is represented in a table or a database. There are lots of ways that data is encoded. For example, there are many ways to represent gender in a database. Gender can be represented by:

Male, female

M,F

1,0

X,Y

And there are probably many other ways to represent gender.

All of these ways of representing gender can be easily translated into a common format. Ironically, the choice of the final format hardly matters. What is important is that there be a single format that represents all the sources of text and data.

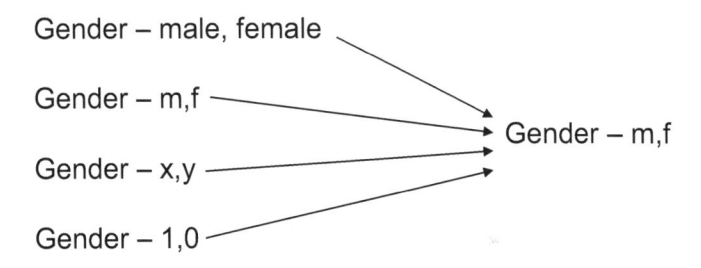

Figure 23: Unify encoding of data.

Measurement

Databases contain lots of different kinds of data. Some types of data require a parameter governing the dimensions of the data. As a simple example, suppose a doctor wants to measure the healing rate of a wound made by surgery. The wound is measured each week to ensure that healing is occurring.

The doctor can measure the wound in many ways, such as by inches, centimeters, feet, etc. To place text into an analytical database, there needs to be a single type of measurement: centimeters. It doesn't particularly matter what measurement has been chosen. Centimeters is as good as any other measurement. What matters is that a single measurement be chosen.

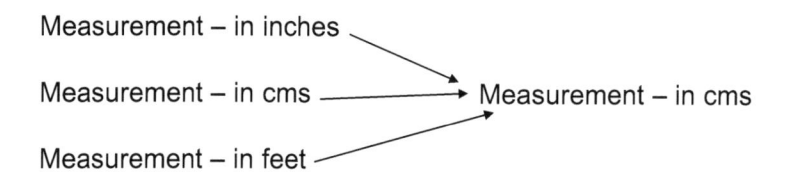

Measurement – in inches
Measurement – in cms → Measurement – in cms
Measurement – in feet

Figure 24: Unify measurement of data.

Language

Medical documents come in many languages. It is necessary to consolidate the different languages into a common language suitable for analysis.

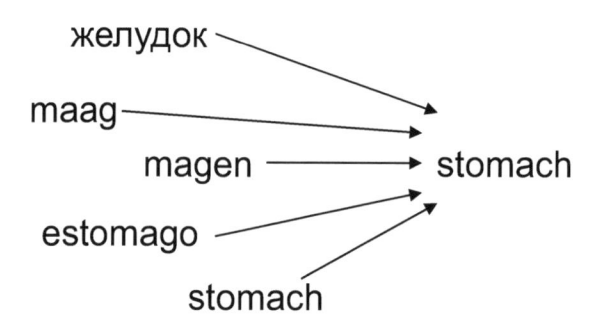

желудок
maag
magen → stomach
estomago
stomach

Figure 25: Unify the language of data.

Common structure

Different kinds of data can be structured in many different ways.

A simple example is the structuring of date. Date can be structured as:

Month/date/year
Year/day/month
Date spelled out

The actual final specification for the format of date really doesn't matter. What matters is that all the ways that date can be specified be consolidated into a single format. Of course, the structuring of date is only the tip of the iceberg. Other common fields that are structured include:

- Telephone number
- National identity number (Social Security number)
- Passport number
- Driver's license number

And so forth.

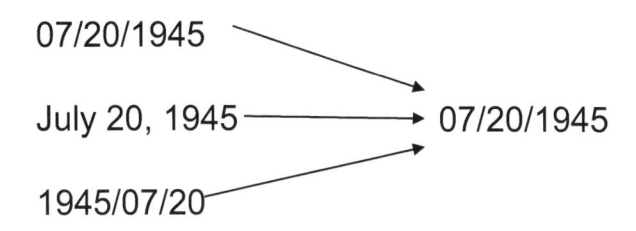

07/20/1945
July 20, 1945 → 07/20/1945
1945/07/20

Figure 26: Unify the structure of data.

Spelling

There are different spelling practices around the world. The English spell the word "color" as "colour". The words mean exactly the same thing. But the words are spelled differently. The analyst doing a study needs to have a singular spelling of the word. In addition, there are common misspellings of a word. These misspellings need to be corrected as well.

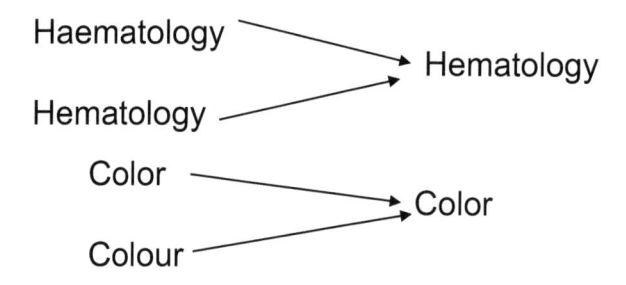

Figure 27: Unify the spelling of data.

Grouping similar objects

One of the most powerful things an analyst can do is to group similar objects together. In other instances, it is seen that exact occurrences of data have been grouped together. But it is also useful to group close but not identical objects together as well.

For example, the medications Aspirin, Advil and Tylenol have been grouped together as analgesics. Tylenol and Aspirin have some important medical differences. But they are also used for the same purpose by a wide population. Therefore, they can be grouped together under a generic classification for most analytical purposes.

Grouping like objects together is valuable because the analyst can refer to the drugs individually or by their classification. The ability to refer to general classification of text and data is extremely useful for the analyst doing research.

Aspirin
Advil ⟶ Analgesic
Tylenol

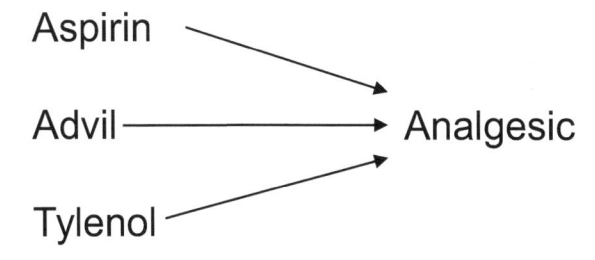

Figure 28: Unify the classification of similar objects.

Acronyms

The medical profession (and airline pilots) are quite adept at building and using acronyms. The proliferation of acronyms by the medical profession is no surprise, given the complexity and the specialization of medical vocabulary. To do research properly, the analyst must know the meanings of the acronyms.

Complicating matters is the fact that one specialty of medicine will use the same acronym as another specialty of medicine but the acronym will mean something different for each specialty.

In any case the analyst needs to have the acronym spelled out in detail in order to do a cogent analysis. If an acronym is widely used and understood on its own, then there may be no need to translate the meaning. Everyone understands what an ICU is. But many medical acronyms are not widely used and are not widely known. These more specific acronyms need to be clarified for the analyst to be able to include the acronym in the study.

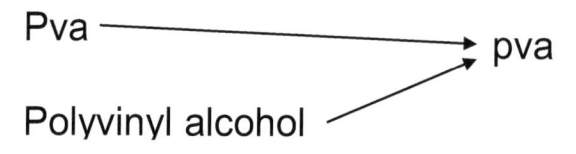

Pva ⟶ pva
Polyvinyl alcohol ⟶

Figure 29: Unify the acronyms that are used.

Homographs

In the same vein as acronyms are homographs. A homograph is a word that is spelled the same but has different meanings according to who spoke the word.

As a simple example, consider the term "ha". Suppose the term "ha" is encountered in the reading of doctor's notes. How should the term "ha" be interpreted? The answer is that the term should be interpreted according to the profession of the doctor who wrote the term. If a cardiologist wrote the term, the term means heart attack. If a general practitioner wrote the term, the term means headache. If an endocrinologist wrote the term, the meaning would be hepatitis A.

To make the proper interpretation of a homograph, it is necessary to know who wrote or spoke the term. The analyst doing research from a database needs to know the proper or intended interpretation of the homograph.

Ha – heart attack – cardiologist

Ha – headache – general practitioner

Ha – hepatitis a - endocrinologist

Figure 30: Unify homographic data.

Calculations

One source document displays 130 pounds. Another document contains 59 kilograms. In fact, 130 pounds is the same weight as 59 kilograms. There needs to be a singular representation of the weight of a person.

130 pounds → 130 pounds
59 kgs →

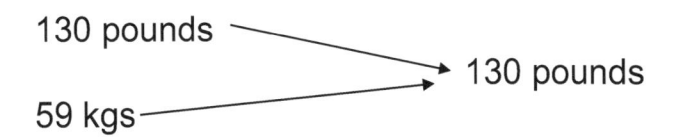

Figure 31: Unify the measurement of data.

Further elucidation

On occasion, it is useful to take a written or spoken term and expand its meaning. Take, for example, the text "Envarsus 20 mg daily". This term has two kinds of information embedded in it. There is a drug, Envarsus, and a dosage of 20 mg daily.

It is a great help to the analyst preparing to use this data in an analysis to have this information separated and identified as to the meaning of the different parts of the phrase.

Of course, there is a logical connection between the drug and the dosage that needs to remain intact. However, making the two different kinds of information available to the analyst in the phrase is very valuable.

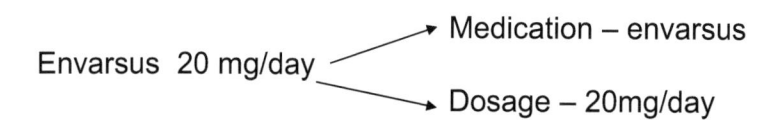

Envarsus 20 mg/day → Medication – envarsus
→ Dosage – 20mg/day

Figure 32: Capture and codify logically related data.

Formatting adjustments

The normal presentation of blood pressure is systolic over diastolic. However, for whatever reason, someone has put diastolic over systolic in a medical record. This formatting error needs to be corrected before the data is presented to the analyst. If not corrected, the error could greatly tangle an analysis.

180/72 systolic/diastolic   180/72 systolic/diastolic

62/128 diastolic/systolic ⟶ 128/62 systolic/diastolic

Figure 33: Unify measurement formats.

Different name for the same object

There are many occasions where there is an object that has more than one name. This is true for medications, procedures, and a whole host of other objects.

The analyst needs to connect these physically separate descriptions but logically singular occurrences of words. One statement of the object needs to arrive in the database. As an example, consider the drug furosemide. Family physicians use the term furosemide, while hospitals use the term Lasix. Yet furosemide and Lasix are exactly the same thing.

This discrepancy needs to be adjusted before reaching the database.

Furosemide ⟶ Furosemide
Lasix ⟶

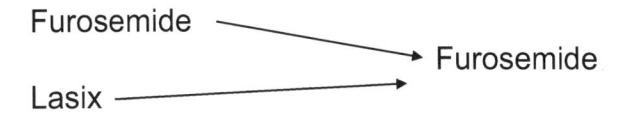

Figure 34: The same object has two different names.

In summary

The net effect of unifying text and data is to create a database that is "clean" for the analyst to use. When data and text are not unified, they are not clean. The cleanliness of the database saves the analyst huge amounts of time. Furthermore, a clean database prevents errors that might otherwise have occurred.

Any one of the corrections and unifications that have been discussed are not particularly difficult to correct. The challenge is that all of these corrections must be made at the same time: at the moment that the data is ingested and loaded into the analytical database.

Given that the payoff in doing text analytics against medical data is in the analysis that is done, anything that can be done to improve the speed, efficiency, and accuracy of the analysis is a positive step forward.

Chapter 6

Building the Database

Once the medical records have been gathered and passed through ingestion, it is now time to process those records and load into a database. At this point, the medical records are in an electronic format that is acceptable to textual ETL.

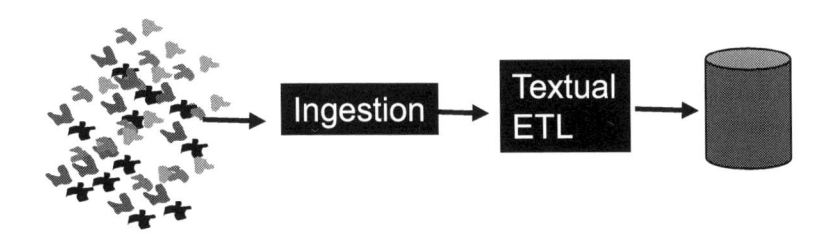

Figure 35: Creating the database.

The basic interface

The start to creating that database by textual ETL is to locate the contextualization software. We will use Datavox as an example in this chapter. Once located, you will see a simple screen. Datavox has a simple, easy-to-use screen that governs its usage.

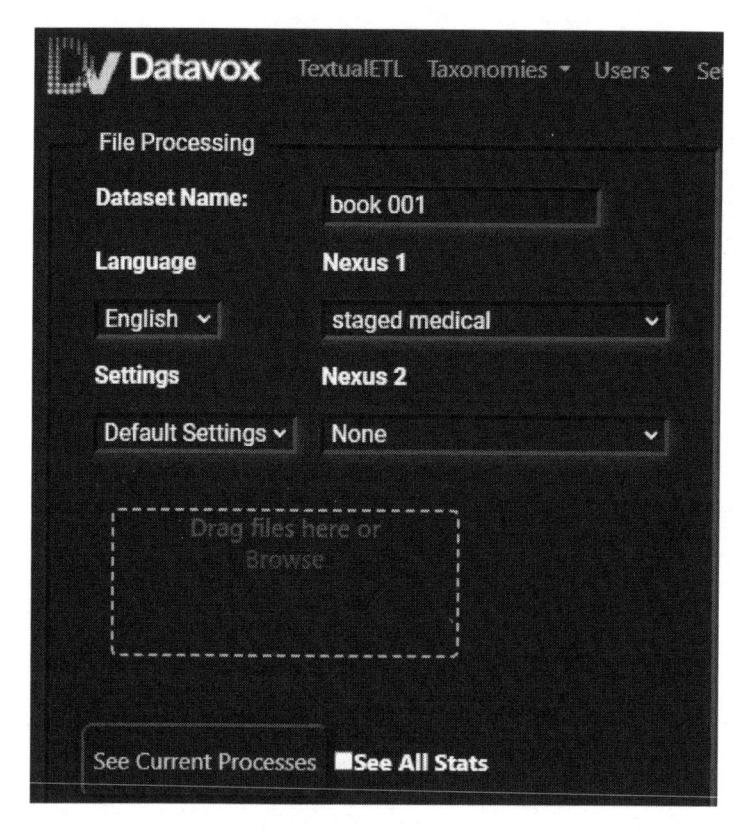

Figure 36: The basic interface.

Once the Datavox screen has been activated, you are ready to create your database from medical records.

Simple questions

There are some simple questions that need to be answered by the analyst in order for Datavox to proceed. The first question is about the language in which the database is to be processed. This refers to the language of the documents. The output database will be in the same language as the input.

There are a number of choices of languages. From time to time, Datavox adds new languages. In Figure 36, we chose English.

If the input documents are not in one of the languages that Datavox supports, the medical records can be translated into one of the languages that Datavox supports before processing. Or, if the medical records are in one of the languages supported by Datavox, they can simply be directly entered into textual ETL.

The second step is to select the category of the documents. In the case of medical records, the category that is selected in Figure 36 is "staged medical". "Staged" refers to the fact that there are many components to the category of medical records. There are medications, procedures, diseases, and so forth. Each of these categories are staged into a single category. The different sub categories are staged together to create a final large category of information.

The next step is to choose a name for the output. This name will be used so that the analyst can recognize the database created when it is released to the system. The name can be anything meaningful to the analyst. In Figure 36, we chose "book 001" to identify the output from textual ETL.

The next step is to choose the medical records that will be processed. This is done by clicking the "browse" button. When the browse button is selected, a panel shows the documents that can be selected.

Some of the considerations here are the quantity of the documents selected and the format of those documents. The format of the documents must conform to the document types that textual ETL supports. As a rule, the document format is chosen when the text enters the ingestion process.

The whole process of sending a medical record into execution takes just seconds. The interface used for Datavox was designed to be as simple to use as an ATM machine. No consultants are required. No special processing or programming is required.

The speed of processing is commensurate with the number of documents processed. A few documents will be processed very quickly. A large number of documents will require more time. If there is a need for a greater processing speed, the workload can be divided among multiple machines. As a rule, one machine can process about three pages per second. If a greater speed is needed, adding more machines is a simple matter. For example, if one machine can process three pages per second, then ten machines can process 30 pages per second. From a technical standpoint, there is effectively no upper limit to the processing speed.

The Datavox database

The Datavox database that is produced can easily be converted to industry-standard databases such as Oracle, SQL Server, DB2, Teradata, and so forth. There are no restrictions as to which target database can be utilized.

Adjusting the vocabulary

The taxonomies that are used contain the common words used in the medical community. They do not contain every medical word that exists. If it turns out that there is a need to add one or more words to the taxonomy, that is easy to do. However, it should be noted that if a word is added to the taxonomy used by Datavox and it is desired to have that word used in a database that has already been created, it is necessary to go back and recreate the database to include the word that has been added.

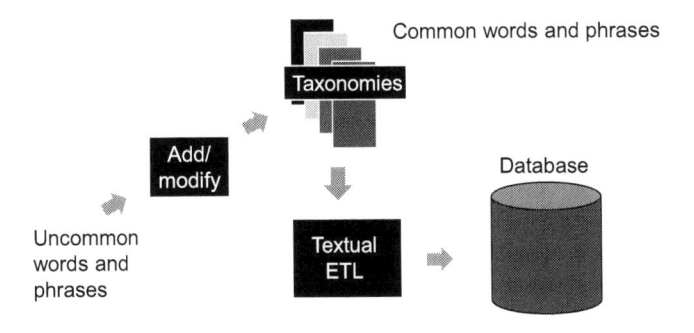

Figure 37: Medical taxonomies already include all commonly used words in medicine. However, if there is a need to add other words, that is not a problem.

The processing done by Datavox can be done either on the cloud or on premise. If done on premise, the organization that manages the off site processing is in charge of the processing. This requires training. No system management is needed if the processing is done on the cloud.

It is noteworthy that no information is stored in the cloud after processing. Once processing occurs on the cloud, the input and the output are sent back to the owners of the information. It is also worth noting that the output is sent directly to the party that instigated the request for processing.

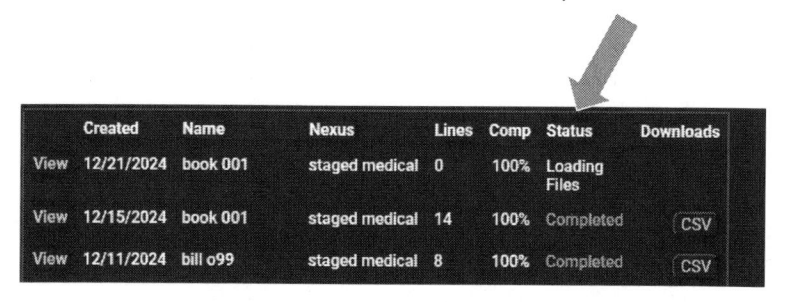

	Created	Name	Nexus	Lines	Comp	Status	Downloads
View	12/21/2024	book 001	staged medical	0	100%	Loading Files	
View	12/15/2024	book 001	staged medical	14	100%	Completed	CSV
View	12/11/2024	bill o99	staged medical	8	100%	Completed	CSV

Figure 38: Once the processing is complete, the system sends a message back to the control screen. The message appears beneath the status bar.

Once the processing is complete, it is possible for the analyst to send the output to themself. This is done by pressing the csv button. Upon pressing the csv button, that output is downloaded to the original instigator.

A closer look at the output data

Figure 39 shows the database that has been produced. At first glance, there are many types of data found in the database. However, many of the data fields are for operators and systems programmers. Only a few columns of data are useful to the medical records analyst.

URL	Source	SubSource	Extention	Nexus	Area	Class	Word	RootWord	Location	FileSize	Sentence	Level	ForDate	WordType	Negations	FirstNega	FirstNega	Trigger	CenterInfo	Classifica	Language
	patient 00	patient 00	txt	date text	Found Da	D/M/####	27/09/193	9/27/1939	57	8657	9		#######	Text of Da	0	1					
	patient 00	patient 00	txt	staged me	lib med dk	dermatolc	gender	gender	80	8657	15	1	#######	Classifica	0	1					English
	patient 00	patient 00	txt	staged me	lib med gi	diet	diet	diet	182	8657	30	1	#######	Classifica	0	-1		-		-	English
	patient 00	patient 00	txt	staged me	lib med or	provider	nutritionis	nutritionis	244	8657	37	1	#######	Classifica	0	-1		-		-	English
	patient 00	patient 00	txt	staged me	lib med ic	icu	icu	icu	280	8657	46	1	#######	Classifica	0	-1		-		-	English
	patient 00	patient 00	txt	staged me	lib med dk	dermatolc	developm	developm	302	8657	49	1	#######	Classifica	0	-1		-		-	English
	patient 00	patient 00	txt	staged me	lib med ic	icu	icu	icu	334	8657	52	1	#######	Classifica	0	1					English
	patient 00	patient 00	txt	staged me	lib med di	disease	pneumon	pneumon	342	8657	55	1	#######	Classifica	0	1					English
	patient 00	patient 00	txt	staged me	lib med de	dermatolc	conjuncti	conjuncti	407	8657	61	1	#######	Classifica	0	-1		-		-	English
	patient 00	patient 00	txt	staged me	lib med pe	pediatrics	conjuncti	conjuncti	407	8657	61	1	#######	Classifica	0	-1		-		-	English
	patient 00	patient 00	txt	staged me	lib med dk	dermatolc	intertrigin	intertrigin	449	8657	64	1	#######	Classifica	0	-1		-		-	English
	patient 00	patient 00	txt	staged me	lib med m	kidney	nystatin	nystatin	492	8657	64	1	#######	Classifica	0	-1		-		-	English
	patient 00	patient 00	txt	staged me	lib med de	dermatolc	topical	topical	514	8657	64	1	#######	Classifica	0	1					English
	patient 00	patient 00	txt	staged me	lib med de	dermatolc	topical	topical	523	8657	64	1	#######	Classifica	0	1					English
	patient 00	patient 00	txt	staged me	lib med m	kidney	nystatin	nystatin	531	8657	64	1	#######	Classifica	0	-1		-		-	English
	patient 00	patient 00	txt	date text	Found Da	D/M	5-Apr	5/4/2024	576	8657	67		#######	Text of Da	0	-1					
	patient 00	patient 00	txt	staged me	lib med m	general	azithromy	azithromy	585	8657	67	1	#######	Classifica	0	-1		-		-	English
	patient 00	patient 00	txt	date text	Found Da	D/M	5-Apr	5/4/2024	667	8657	67		#######	Text of Da	0	1					
	patient 00	patient 00	txt	staged me	lib med pe	pathology	diuresis	diuresis	669	8657	71	1	#######	Classifica	0	1					English
	patient 00	patient 00	txt	staged me	lib med dk	body	oral	oral	782	8657	80	1	#######	Classifica	0	-1		-		-	English
	patient 00	patient 00	txt	staged me	lib med gi	diet	diet	diet	787	8657	80	1	#######	Classifica	0	-1		-		-	English
	patient 00	patient 00	txt	staged me	lib med pe	pathology	diuresis	diuresis	796	8657	84	1	#######	Classifica	0	-1		-		-	English
	patient 00	patient 00	txt	staged me	lib med ca	condition	murmurs	murmur	858	8657	92	1	#######	Classifica	0	-1		-		-	English
	patient 00	patient 00	txt	staged me	lib med te	body	abdomen	abdomen	909	8657	96	1	#######	Classifica	0	1					English
	patient 00	patient 00	txt	staged me	lib med dr	dermatolc	flaccid	flaccid	939	8657	95	1	#######	Classifica	0	1					English
	patient 00	patient 00	txt	staged me	lib med de	dermatolc	perfused	perfuse	971	8657	98	1	#######	Classifica	0	-1		-		-	English
	patient 00	patient 00	txt	staged me	lib med ki	kidney	edema	edema	988	8657	98	1	#######	Classifica	0	-1		-		-	English

Figure 39: The database that has been produced.

The columns of data that are of interest to the medical records analyst are shown in Figure 40.

The first column of data that is of interest is the patient record column. The patient record column holds the patient's record number. It does not hold any personal identification information, such as name or Social Security number. There are multiple occurrences of the patient id because multiple words in the patient record have found their way into the database. Each word that has been found in the medical record has encountered a match in the taxonomy. The result is that textual ETL has created a record in the output database for the matching word.

source	class	word	rootword	location
patient 001.txt	dermatology	gender	gender	80
patient 001.txt	diet	diet	diet	182
patient 001.txt	provider	nutritionist	nutritionist	244
patient 001.txt	icu	icu	icu	280
patient 001.txt	dermatology	developments	development	302
patient 001.txt	icu	icu	icu	334
patient 001.txt	disease	pneumonia	pneumonia	342
patient 001.txt	dermatology	conjunctivitis	conjunctivitis	407
patient 001.txt	pediatrics	conjunctivitis	conjunctivitis	407
patient 001.txt	dermatology	intertriginous	intertriginous	449
patient 001.txt	kidney	nystatin	nystatin	492
patient 001.txt	dermatology	topical	topical	514
patient 001.txt	dermatology	topical	topical	523
patient 001.txt	kidney	nystatin	nystatin	531
patient 001.txt	general	azithromycin	azithromycin	585
patient 001.txt	pathology	diuresis	diuresis	669
patient 001.txt	body	oral	oral	782
patient 001.txt	diet	diet	diet	787
patient 001.txt	pathology	diuresis	diuresis	796
patient 001.txt	condition	murmurs	murmur	898
patient 001.txt	body	abdomen	abdomen	909
patient 001.txt	dermatology	flaccid	flaccid	930
patient 001.txt	dermatology	perfused	perfuse	971
patient 001.txt	kidney	edema	edema	988
patient 001.txt	condition	edema	edema	988
patient 001.txt	dermatology	dependent	dependent	1088
patient 001.txt	icu	mechanical ventil	mechanical vent	1101

Figure 40: The portion of the database that is of interest.

The second column is the byte column. The byte column is the byte address in the medical record where the word that has been matched appears. In other words, if the byte is 437 for a word in the medical record and the record id is patient90, the word found will appear at byte 437 in the source document. Having the record id and the byte available ensures that the database can always be tied to the document in a very specific manner. This capability is useful if there ever is an issue with the integrity or source of the data.

The next column of interest is the actual word itself. The word exists in the source document, and the taxonomy has been used to process the data. The word is spelled exactly as it has been found in the document.

The fourth column of interest is the taxonomy source column. This column tells the analyst the context of the word that has been matched.

If there is a large amount of data to be processed, it is noteworthy that the output of different executions of textual ETL can be combined. Nothing special must be done to combine the data into a single database. The output simply must be collected and gathered to form a single database.

> Once data has been passed through textual ETL and has been aggregated if necessary, the database that has been created is ready for analytical processing.

In summary

Once text has been ingested, unified, and placed into an electronic format, the text is ready for processing. If there are large amounts of text, the text needs to be divided into smaller subsets and each subset is processed individually. If necessary, more than one machine can process the text.

At the end of processing, the output databases are combined into a single database. The text, when prepared, is sent to textual ETL.

Textual ETL has an interface similar to an ATM. If you can use an ATM, you can use textual ETL. Textual ETL requires four basic pieces:

- The language processing is to take place in
- The topic of the text to be processed
- The identifier used to locate the output data
- The files to be processed

Chapter 7

Exploration

There are many people to whom medical records are valuable. They are valuable to the doctor, to the patient, to the lab technician, and many others. Individually, medical records have worth to many different people. Taken collectively, medical records are valuable to the researcher looking for answers where answers are often hidden. When viewed collectively, medical records open up vistas that could otherwise be impossible to view.

To unlock the secrets hidden in a collection of medical records, it is necessary to employ a discipline that can best be described as the process of exploration. The exploration process takes place meticulously and provides a detailed analysis of many medical records.

Exploration and clinical trials

The exploration process fundamentally differs from the exploration done in the clinical trial process. The main difference between the two methods of exploration and analysis is that the exploration of medical records is based on a historical description of the journey of many patients. The description of the journey as described in medical records cannot be carefully controlled. The exploration analyst of medical records must work with medical record data as it was recorded. You cannot go back in time and recreate the treatment and circumstances of a medical record that has not been recorded. So, when exploring medical records, the analyst must work with whatever information has been recorded, no more and no less.

The good news is that the exploration analyst has unlimited records from which to choose. Any legitimate medical record can be considered and used for the exploration. And there are a lot of medical records.

Another piece of good news is that the exploration analyst of medical records is free to explore as much data as possible and as many types of data that make sense. There is nothing to limit the range of the variables that can be explored other than the fact that the exploration is restricted to the data that has been captured on the record.

Clinical trials operate in a very different mode of exploration. While it is true that clinical trials are a form of exploration, they are very different from those done on medical records. In a clinical trial, there is a need to control the subjects and the circumstances surrounding the patient selected for the trial carefully and conduct the clinical trial according to scientific research standards.

> *Whereas the exploration process of medical records is essentially uncontrolled, the clinical trial process is carefully controlled.*

In accordance with these constraints, clinical trials usually involve only a small audience of participants, while exploratory analyses of medical records can involve a huge number of participants.

Computer systemization

From the exploration analysis of medical records, a computerized systemization of patients' data is often used to take advantage of the information that has been gleaned. There simply are so many medical records involved that a computer is needed to manage the volume of those records. There are several approaches to building a computerized system. There are basically two elements that drive the way a computerized system is built:

- **Requirements**. Are the requirements for the system known before the system is built?

- **Process**. Is there a methodical way to create an architecture for the system to be built once the requirements for the system are known?

These elements of building a computerized system can be illustrated by some examples.

In the 1890's, when the French statistician and demographer, Jacques Bertillon, set out to build a system for classifying causes of death, he wanted to standardize why people died so that better research could be conducted to curb unneeded deaths. When the United States adopted this classification in 1898, they saw the value in using a common classification system. In the 1980's, the World Health Organization (WHO) took on the current International Classifications of Diseases' tenth revision (ICD-10), so that all medical decisions can be specifically classified globally. This new set of codes consists of around 87,000 codes as opposed to ICD-9, which had around 14,000 codes. The United States, for HIPPA and Medicare billing, adopted another classification system used for billing called Current Procedural Terminology (CPT). This system was paired with the ICD system to verify that the medical industry was properly billing the government.

Coding is needed for conformance to insurance requirements for reimbursement. Furthermore, a well-established method for properly doing ICD and CPT coding was created. Any new system built for this purpose is well-defined before the system is conceived because the coding is set forth by laws.

The challenge for this kind of system is automating the steps of proper ICD and CPT coding. Another challenge is training medical professionals to properly use this system. The third challenge is with so many very specific codes, it is physically impossible for humans to properly code ICD or CPT codes for the actual issues with the patients. So, the requirements are known, but the process, although legally defined, is impossible to follow.

Now consider the work done by Jonas Salk. Dr Salk knew the requirements before he set out to find medicine applicable to polio. However, there was no roadmap for developing a treatment for combatting polio. The requirements were known, but the process was not defined. Dr Salk had to proceed in a trial-and-error manner.

To illustrate an instance where neither the requirements were known nor the process of developing a system was known, consider COVID. When COVID appeared, no one knew anything about COVID and there certainly was no effective treatment for it. When research for COVID began, it was more of a general fact-finding mission rather than a mission searching for a cure.

Exploration in the face of no known requirements is often very unfocused. Anything and everything that might be relevant to the knowledge about the condition being studied is fair game. Exploration in the face of unknown requirements is a general-purpose fact-finding mission.

Clinical trials are done in the face of very known, very controlled requirements. Exploration in the face of known requirements is focused, not a general search of any relevant facts that might have been captured.

	Requirements	Process
ICD 9 coding	known	known
Salk/polio	known	unknown
COVID	unknown	unknown

Figure 41: System development can proceed down very different paths.

There is an interesting relationship between exploration in the face of unknown requirements and exploration in the face of known requirements. An exploration of unknown requirements can lead to the understanding of what to study in a clinical trial. Insights are gained in an exploration of unknown requirements. Those insights then shape how to conduct and shape clinical trials that further define, in great detail, elements that lead to a cure or an effective treatment for a medical condition.

The potential of no resolution

When embarking on an exploration of any kind, where requirements are either known or unknown, the analyst must recognize that the analysis may achieve no results. Furthermore, the analyst must recognize that the length and steps of the exploration cannot be ascertained before the exploration commences. In an iterative process, the next step of the analysis is ascertained by looking at the insights resulting from the current iteration of the analysis.

Consider an example to understand how the analysis of unknown facts can proceed.

Once there was an automobile airbag company located in Arizona. Airbags are embedded in a car and explode, protecting the driver and the passenger in a collision. Airbags are interesting in that they must stand ready for usage years after they have been developed. Yet they still have to be ready for usage at a moment's notice.

A person driving a twenty-year-old car expects the same airbag performance as a person who has driven an automobile fresh off the dealership car lot. Airbags must be prepared for immediate and emergency usage for a long time. Furthermore, an airbag protects the life of the driver and the passenger. A failure of the airbag during a collision can be catastrophic.

At the center of the airbag is an explosion device that inflates the airbag on the occasion of an accident. The explosive device consists of an encasement of the explosive, the firing pin, and the explosive itself.

It was noticed by the manufacturer of the airbag that the stability of the explosive was very unstable. The explosive, which was mixed at the plant in Arizona, would one day be very reliable and stable, but the next day, it would be very unreliable and prone to random explosions.

This presented a real problem for the airbag company. The unstable explosive was detrimental to the quality of manufacturing. And the instability of the explosion was dangerous to employees as well. As long as the explosive placed in the airbag was unstable, the manufacturer had a real problem.

The airbag company set out to find out why there was such a variance in the quality and stability of the mixing of the explosive. By finding out the cause of the problem, the airbag company could then determine a solution.

The first step in the analysis by the engineers that were charged with resolving the explosive problem was to develop a chart of the pattern of the instability of the explosive. The chart depicting the instability of the explosive looked like the diagram in Figure 42.

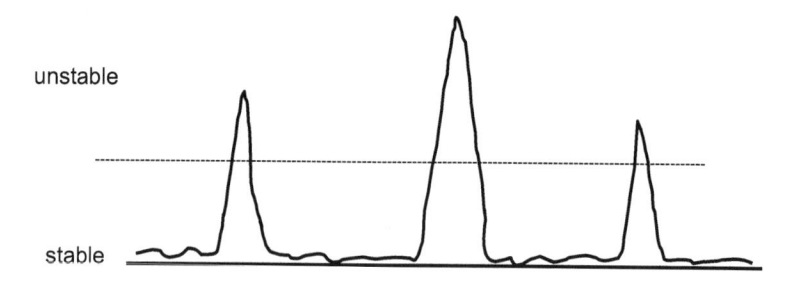

Figure 42: The pattern of instability of the explosive.

The next step in the analysis was to determine the cause of the variation. It was at this point that the airbag company had to do some exploration.

The engineer at the airbag company had the intuition to look to the supplier of the base ingredients of the explosive. This was a natural place to look. If the suppliers of the base materials making up the explosive could be shown to be supplying faulty raw products, that might explain why the explosive was unstable. However, the raw ingredients were tested and there was no indication that the supplier had supplied anything other than a high-quality product. There simply was no correlation between the quality of the raw material being delivered and the incidence of instability.

The next suspect in the exploration process was the mixing process. The raw goods used to create the explosive arrived at the airbag plant and were mixed at the airbag plant. Engineers examined the mixing process and could find no relationship between the mixing process and the periods of instability.

Next the engineers at the airbag company started to inspect the storage of the explosive. Here, they found no correlation between the periods of instability and the storage of the explosive.

At this point, the engineers had exhausted the normal culprits that might have contributed to the instability of the explosive.

Grasping at straws, the engineers started to see if there was some correlation between the workers mixing or handling the explosives and the periods of instability. They looked for a worker who might not be conducting their job properly. No correlation was found.

At this point, the engineers could not explain the instability in mixing the explosives. The instability and the danger remained.

The engineers looked at every possible thing that might have caused the instability of the explosive. At this point, the engineers looked at factors that seemed farfetched.

Then one day, on an intuitive hunch, an engineer decided to map the humidity in the air to the pattern of instability of the explosive. The air in Arizona is normally very dry air. But every now and then, a current of moist Pacific Ocean air finds its way over the Baja and the desert, and the humidity in Arizona changes. These humidity changes were mapped. Then the pattern in the changes in humidity were mapped against the patterns of instability of the explosive. The mapping is shown in Figure 43.

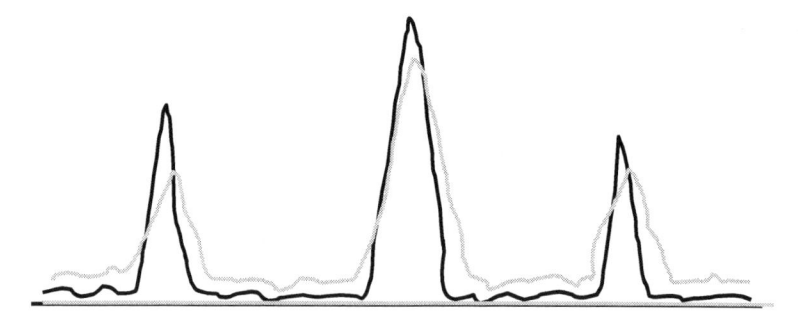

Figure 43: Fitting the humidity versus the instability patterns.

The mapping was nearly perfect. The engineers had discovered the cause of the instability of the explosive. Once the effect of humidity was disclosed, it became obvious that humidity greatly influenced how explosives were mixed and created. But in the beginning, this relationship was unknown.

Lessons learned from an exploration

So what can this true story about exploration processing in the face of unknown facts tell us? There are, in fact, a number of lessons:

- **Lesson 1.** Exploration is often unintuitive. Sometimes intuition and experience lead to satisfying results. Sometimes intuition and experience do not lead in a productive direction. The analyst must be open to even far-fetched ideas and be prepared to explore seemingly unproductive paths.

- **Lesson 2.** In even the most successful explorations, there will be false turns and "rabbit holes" that do not lead anywhere productive. This is simply the nature of exploring unknown vistas.

- **Lesson 3.** In the final analysis, an exploration may not yield any positive results or any results at all. The analyst must be prepared to face this fact of reality. However, documenting what exploration has been done but has not been productive can be important in itself. Future analysts will know where not to turn to for future explorations.

- **Lesson 4.** In other cases, exploration of unknown circumstances can produce very valuable results.

Different approaches to exploration

Once an exploration of medical records commences, different approaches can be taken to exploring the data. One of the approaches is called the drill-down approach. In the drill-down approach, the analyst starts with a simple pairing of two likely variables and produces a correlative analysis. The analyst then analyzes the correlation that has been produced. In the next iteration of the drill-down approach, the analyst adds another variable to the equation and analyzes the correlation of the new variable that has been added. If the new variable correlates, then another likely variable is added to the equation. The drill-down process continues until the desired result is obtained.

How many cases of COVID did we have?
How many cases of COVID were men?
How many of male COVID patients were over 70?
How many male COVID patients over 70 were smokers?

Figure 44: Drill-down exploration (linear).

Another approach to drill down processing can be called the non-linear approach to drill down processing. In the non-linear approach, the different iterations of the analysis do not necessarily build from one variable to the next. Instead, the variables that are investigated are varied from one iteration to the next in an unrelated manner.

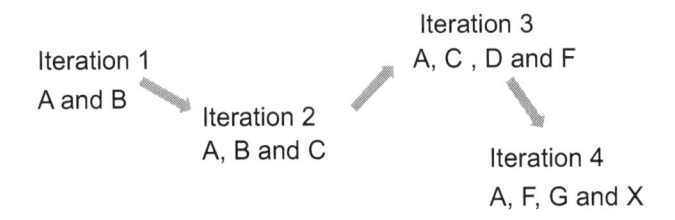

```
                              Iteration 3
        Iteration 1           A, C , D and F
        A and B
                   ↘  Iteration 2   ↗              ↘
                      A, B and C            Iteration 4
                                            A, F, G and X
```

Figure 45: Drill-down exploration (non-linear).

Another approach to exploration processing is the drill-across approach. In the drill-across approach different variations of the same variable are used on each iteration of analysis.

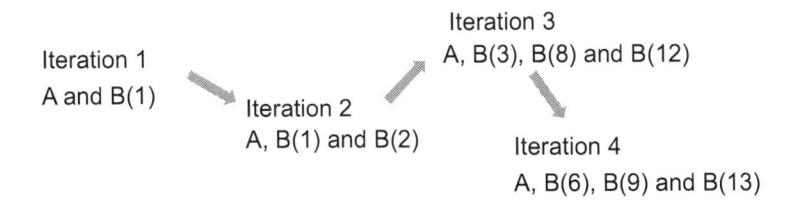

```
                              Iteration 3
        Iteration 1           A, B(3), B(8) and B(12)
        A and B(1)
                   ↘  Iteration 2      ↗              ↘
                      A, B(1) and B(2)        Iteration 4
                                              A, B(6), B(9) and B(13)
```

Figure 46: Drill-down exploration (drill-across).

Scatter diagrams

One technique to track an analysis's results is called the scatter diagram or scatter plot approach. In the scatter diagram approach, the results that are obtained are plotted on a two-dimensional graph. After enough results have been obtained, a line is run through the results using a calculation called the least squares method. This line is created to reduce the sum of the squared distances of each of the plotted points from the line and will pass through the point (x,y). The line gives the predicted points for each X given Y. The problem with the least squares approach is that it is based on averages and standard deviations and can be influenced by points far from the line, called outliers.

Since the line is a perfect predictor, an often more useful approach is to evaluate a graph that shows how far away each of the actual points is from the predicted points. This graph is called the residuals graph and shows the range of observations where you can trust the prediction and the areas where you might expect higher or lower results. An issue with this approach is that it only deals in two dimensions or with two quantitative variables.

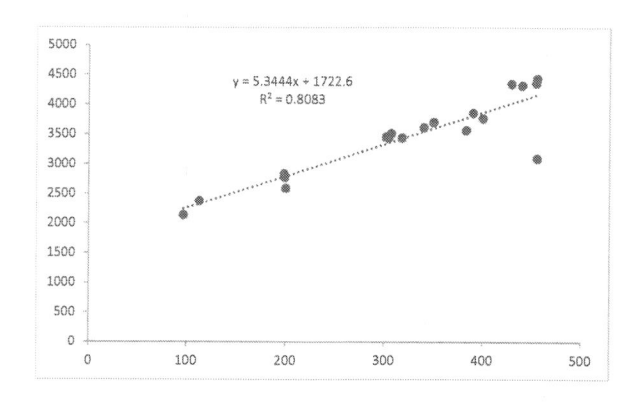

Figure 47: The pattern of observations portrayed by a scatter diagram with trendline.

Correlation

One of the most important factors in comparing two or more variables against each other is what is known as correlation. In correlation, the relationship of one variable to the next is ascertained. There is much insight to be gained when the relationship of variables is compared in light of the correlation of the variables to each other.

The squared correlation coefficient, known as r^2, is the percentage of one variable's movement that can be explained by the movement of another variable. Since r is a number from -1 to +1 or -100% to + 100%, r^2 is a number from 0 to +1. One very important thing about correlation is that correlation indicates co-related movement. Correlation does not mean causation.

There are essentially three types of correlative relationships: a positive correlative relationship, a negative correlative relationship, and an unknown (or a non-existent) correlative relationship.

A positive correlative relationship is one where if variable A tends upward, then variable B also trends upward, or if variable A trends downward, then variable B also trends downward. In other words, the variables move in tandem with each other. A negative correlative relationship is one where if variable A trends upward, variable B trends downward, or if variable A trends downward, then variable B trends upward. In a negative correlation, the variables trend in opposite directions.

An unknown correlative relationship is one where there is no known relationship between the trends displayed by the variables. The variables operate in a random manner.

One aspect of correlation is the strength of trending. Where the relationship moves in tandem almost all the time, the strength of the relationship is strong. r^2 is considered strong when it is over 80% mattering the subject. Where the variables move in tandem most of the time but not all of the time, the relationship between the variables is moderate. r^2 is considered moderate when it is over 50% mattering the area.

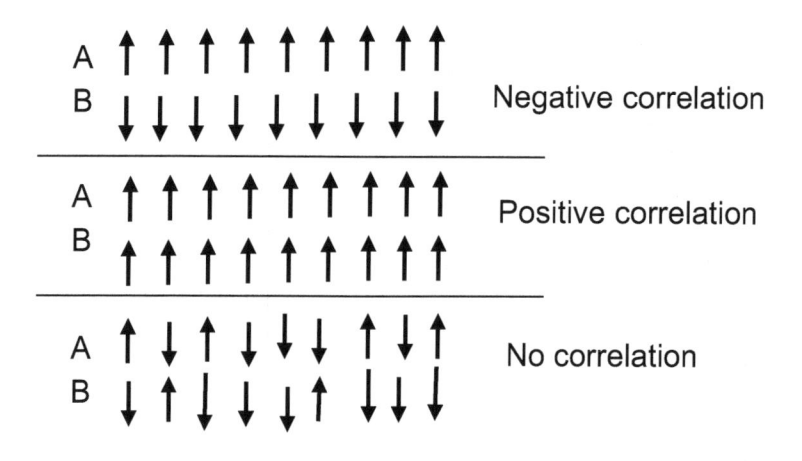

Figure 48: How does A correlate to B?

A Pearson coefficient matrix

One of the most useful ways to measure correlative relationships between variables is through a Pearson coefficient matrix.

In a Pearson coefficient matrix, each variable is measured against each other variable. An independent measurement of each relationship of each variable to each other was found in the study.

In a Pearson coefficient matrix, many variables are measured against each other. The strength of the relationship can be shown by a color. If the color is red, there is a negative correlation of the variables. If the color is green, there is a positive correlation between the two variables. If the color is light red, there is a weak negative relationship between the two variables. If the color is light green, there is a weak positive relationship between the two variables.

The Pearson coefficient matrix shown in the example is for patient records that relate to COVID.

In the Pearson coefficient matrix, it is possible to find:

How COVID relates to smoking
How COVID relates to previously taken medications
How COVID relates to gender
How COVIC relates to education

And so forth.

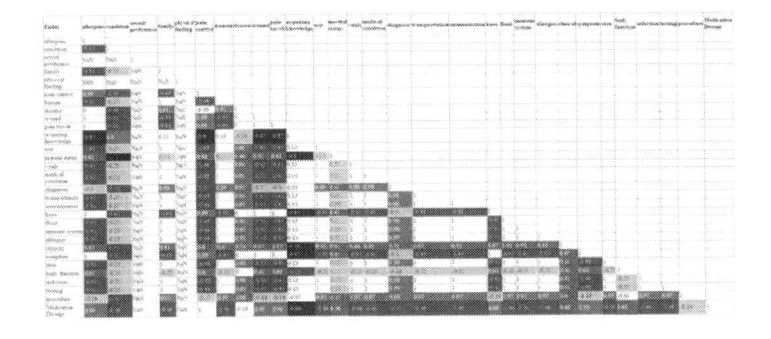

Figure 49: A Pearson coefficient matrix.

The only limitation as to what is not shown in the Pearson coefficient matrix is for the data that is not in the medical record.

Of course, an analysis can be done on many more medical conditions than COVID.

When dealing with correlations, an issue that always arises is whether the relationship between variable A and variable B is a cause or simply a correlation?

There are many things that are correlated but not related in a causal manner. To determine causality, it is necessary to examine the business relationship between variable A and variable B. There is a definite difference between a statistical relationship and business (or reality) relationship.

It is the business relationship (or reality) that determines causality. The statistical relationship between two variables can be merely coincidental. Quite often, people will consider correlation to be causal, when it is something else that is the cause and the variables are a side effect of that situation.

The need for speed

One of the essential, if not the most important essential, aspects of the exploration processing of medical records is the need for speed. The faster an analysis iteration, the more freedom the analyst has.

The biggest impediment to the speed of iterations in the exploration process of medical records is the gathering and preparation of data to load into a database.

All other aspects of the exploration process of medical records are lightning-fast compared to the time needed to gather and process the raw text.

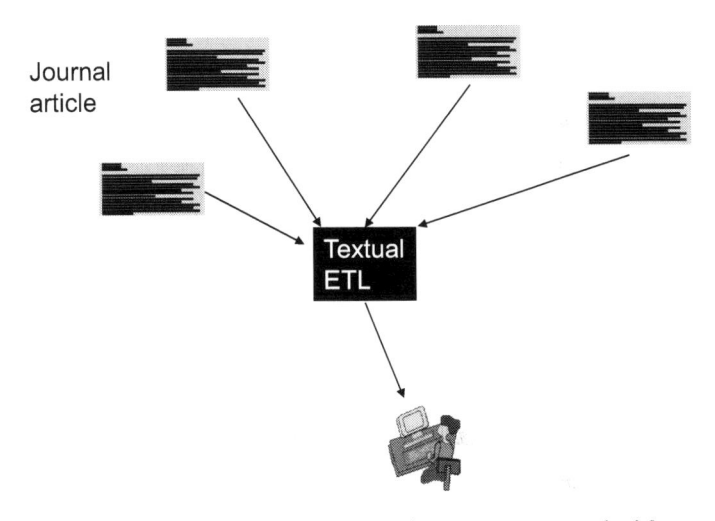

Figure 50: For non-exploration analysis, textual ETL serves as a method for efficiently and accurately searching many studies.

In summary

The exploration process of medical records differs from the process used in clinical trials. With medical records, there is no opportunity for tight control of the participants in the study.

However, with medical records, the study is boundless because there are many medical records to choose from.

The study of medical records is limited to the data captured on the record by the doctor.

The exploration process of medical records is a heuristic process. At the outset, the analyst does not know:

- If anything will ever be found
- How long the study will take
- How many iterations there will be.

The exploration of medical records depends on the ability to have a fast turnaround time in developing one iteration of analysis to the next.

Chapter 8

Analytics

While the process of taking text from medical records in its raw state and turning the medical record text into a database is an interesting and inevitable task, the truth is that the real payoff of analyzing medical record text to the organization is in the analytics that come from the creation and analysis of a textually-founded database. Once the textually-founded database is created, the organization can read and analyze millions of medical documents and lines of text. Finding information from millions of documents is immensely useful in medicine.

Medical records were designed to handle the clinical needs of one patient and one doctor. Medical records in a textual state are not designed to analyze millions of records, as needed by the medical researcher.

In this chapter, the analysis created from a textually-founded medical record database will be done from the single database that was created in an earlier chapter.

Many forms of analysis

The analytics from the textually-founded medical record database can be displayed and analyzed in many forms. In this chapter, the discussion will center on four different common types of analytical tools and forms of analysis:

- A spreadsheet
- A query-based tool
- A dashboard
- A knowledge graph.

When these analytical tools are examined individually, there is always some overlap of functionality between each tool.

There are, however, differences between the analytical tools and approaches to analysis. The emphasis in the analysis done in this chapter is on the differences between the analytical tools, not the similarities of the tools.

Operating from the same database

In this chapter, the same textually-founded medical record database was used for the analysis created by these analytical tools. In that regard, this chapter can be used to compare the different analysis tools. It is noteworthy that the tools discussed do not have all of the tool's features on full display. Also, we focus on the salient differences between the analytical tools, not the similarities.

The database that is used as a foundation for analysis is not a standard database created from structured data. Instead, the database that is used is a database designed for textual data, not structured data.

Textual database versus a structured database

To highlight this difference between the different kinds of databases that can be created, consider the following simple structured database.

The structured database has been constructed from a list of voter registrations. The voter registration list is created, and the structured database is constructed from the voter registration data. Database construction is done thousands of times a day in many different forms.

```
Voter registration —
Bill    Ind  1945  Colorado  male    Caucasian
Sylvia  Dem  1945  Nebraska  female  Native American
Sarah   Rep  1983  Florida           female  Caucasian
Ross    Rep  1947  Colorado  male    Jewish
Juan    Ind  1993  Texas     male    Hispanic
```

Name	location	gender
Bill	Colorado	male
Sarah	Florida	female
Ross	Colorado	male
Sylvia	Colorado	female

Figure 51: The structured database.

The structured database in Figure 51 represents the type of data created many times by designers and analysts in the structured environment. It is familiar to the person with a background in building and managing structured data.

Now consider a text-based database. Suppose the raw text is encountered as shown in Figure 52. The raw text is read and the analysis of the text supplies the words of interest to the database. In addition, the context of the words that have been encountered is captured as well.

As has been discussed when handling text, it is mandatory that both the text and the context of the text be captured as part of the processing of the text.

On Wednesday Bill's boss fired him. Bill got into his Porsche and Took his creel and fishing rod and headed for the Rockies to fish. He took his gun in case he saw a grizzly. He had been expecting his firing to occur but it was still a shock. He needed some time to think things over.

Word	context
Trout	fish
Fire	gun
Fire	termination
Porsche	car type
Rockies	mountain range

Figure 52: a text-based database.

The difference between a structured database and a textual based database is in the location and treatment of the context of the data.

In a structured database, context is found by looking at the column heading. The column for name includes only names. The column for location contains only locations. The column for gender contains only gender, and so forth. The structuring of data and context that has been described is descriptive of the way structured data is organized.

The textual-based database base is quite different. The context for the text encountered is contained in a separate column in the row. A trout is a fish. Someone fired a gun. Someone lost their job. A Porsche is a type of car, and so forth. All of these occurrences of text are placed in a database, along with their context.

When one examines the column name for word, each entry in the column is a word. But there is no uniformity of the contents of the column. A word can be anything. To understand the context of the word, looking at the context column in the same row is necessary. It is there that the context of the word is disclosed.

In the structured database, each row in a column conforms to the name of the row. But in the textual-based database, the contents of the word column conform to nothing. To find the context of the contents of the word column, it is necessary to look at the context column for each row that is encountered.

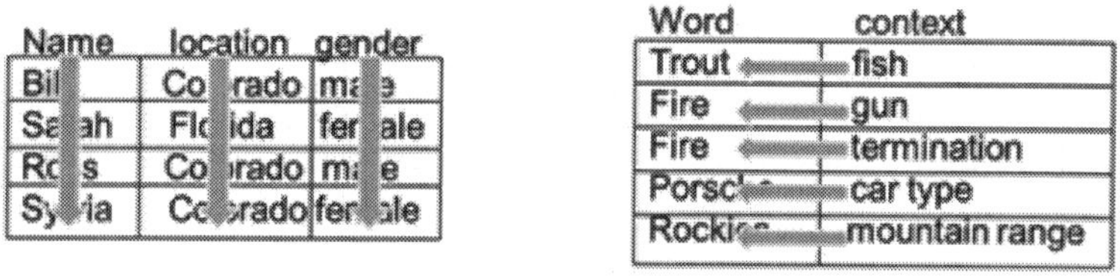

Figure 53: Understanding context.

Different types of analytical tools

The different types of analytical tools described in this chapter are:

- Spreadsheet – Excel
- Knowledge graph – Neo4j
- Dashboard – Tableau
- Query-based – ThoughtSpot

There are, of course, many other analytical tools other than the ones that are discussed. However, these tools are good representatives of their particular type of tool.

There are many different ways to compare the different tools of analysis. Note that the comparison categories are very general and address only the differentiated components of a product.

To get a full disclosure, it is advised that a conversation with a vendor is appropriate.

	visual/ database	static/ dynamic	audience	summary/ detail	query	text adaptive	interface
Excel	database	static	general/ technical	detail	technical	moderate	seamless
Neo4J	visual	dynamic	technical management	detail	graphic	highly	seamless
Tableau	visual	static	management	detail	graphic	moderate	seamless
Thoughtspot	semantic	static	management	summary	semantic	highly	seamless

Figure 54: A thumbnail comparison.

- **Visual/database.** Some products focus on the visualization of results. Other products focus on the display of a database where the user can manipulate that database as they wish. Other products focus on the calculation of a single result.

- **Static/dynamic database.** Some products assume the data sent to them is static and can't be structurally manipulated. Other products focus on the ability to create dynamic relationships for the database that has been supplied.

- **Audience.** Some products have a general audience that can be used by management and technicians. Other products are much more oriented to management. It is noted that almost all of the products can be used by either community. However, there is still an emphasis on one community or the other.

- **Summary/detail.** Some products focus on detailed data analysis. Other products focus on summarized data. Of course, almost all products support some degree of support for both detailed and summary data. The distinction made here is on the primary focus of the product.

- **Query.** All analytical tools support some form of query processing. In some products, the query processing is technical. In other products, the query processing is primarily graphical. In other products, the query processing is very user-friendly and semantic.

- **Text adaptive.** In some products, the expectation is for the database being served to be a structured database. In this case, a textual-based database is awkward or less than optimal to handle. In other products, the expectation is either a structured or textually based database.

- **Interface.** In every case, the interface of getting data from the database to the product is seamless. Both the structured and textual-based databases are in a classical structured format, which is required for access and usage by the product.

Spreadsheet data analysis – Excel

The following figure shows the spreadsheet that has been created from the database that has been supplied.

Sub-Source	Nexus	Area	Class	Word	Location
patient 001	staged medical	lib med dermatology	dermatology	gender	80
patient 001	staged medical	lib med gi	diet	diet	182
patient 001	staged medical	lib med oncology	provider	nutritionist	244
patient 001	staged medical	lib med icu	icu	icu	280
patient 001	staged medical	lib med dermatology	dermatology	developments	302
patient 001	staged medical	lib med icu	icu	icu	334
patient 001	staged medical	lib med disease	disease	pneumonia	342
patient 001	staged medical	lib med dermatology	dermatology	conjunctivitis	407
patient 001	staged medical	lib med pediatrics	pediatrics	conjunctivitis	407
patient 001	staged medical	lib med dermatology	dermatology	intertriginous	449
patient 001	staged medical	lib med medication	kidney	nystatin	492
patient 001	staged medical	lib med dermatology	dermatology	topical	514
patient 001	staged medical	lib med dermatology	dermatology	topical	523
patient 001	staged medical	lib med medication	kidney	nystatin	531
patient 001	date text	Found Date	D/M	5-Apr	578
patient 001	staged medical	lib med medication	general	azithromycin	585
patient 001	date text	Found Date	D/M	5-Apr	607
patient 001	staged medical	lib med pathology	pathology	diuresis	669
patient 001	staged medical	lib med dentistry	body	oral	782

Figure 55: The data is organized so that individual columns can be analyzed.

As an example of what can be analyzed, the analyst could answer such questions as:

- What disease has been encountered the most frequently among the patients at the hospital?
- What class of disease is the most common?
- Has anyone been treated for Japanese encephalitis?
- What dosages for Tylenol have been described?

The analyst can control the direction of the analysis based on the immediate answering of questions. Among other things, spreadsheets are very useful for doing iterative analysis simply because they can be analyzed quickly and in a flexible manner.

However, spreadsheets do not support graphic imaging to any great extent.

The following Excel pivot tables provide examples of analysis that can be performed.

Area	lib med pathology
Row Labels	**Count of Word**
medication	**22**
amine	3
amines	19
pathology	**173**
anastomosis	1
auscultation	5
diuresis	135
hematoma	2

Row Labels	Count of Word
hemiparesis	1
hernia	2
hyperemia	3
infarction	2
oliguria	1
palsy	5
peristalsis	1
peritonitis	1
shock	11
urea	3
Grand Total	195

SubSource	patient fgh
Row Labels	**Count of Word**
lib med oncology	**28**
examine	1
medication	4
oncology	12
provider	2
therapy	9
lib med palliative	**1**
palliative	1
lib med pathology	**13**
pathology	13
lib med rheumatism	**1**
rheumatism	1
lib med urology	**1**
urology	1
Grand Total	**183**

Figure 56: Sample pivot tables.

Genai based query suite – Thoughtspot

ThoughtSpot is a cloud-based analytical tool suite that combines traditional querying and analysis with the power of Generative Artificial Intelligence (GenAI) for users to enter natural-language prompts to gain reporting insights. ThoughtSpot's powerful GenAI platform is called "Spotter", which intuitively takes those questions and instantly converts them into a computer-knowledgeable query.

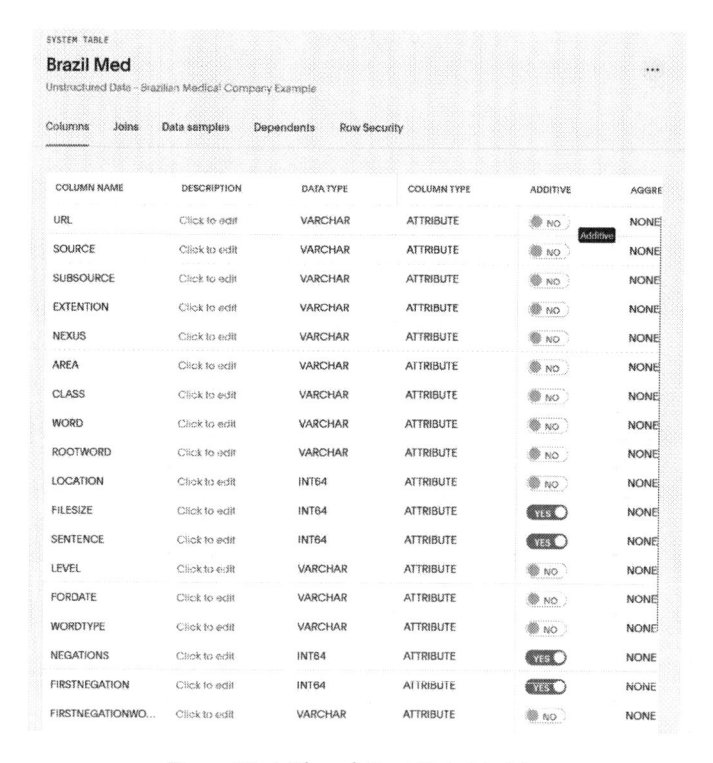

Figure 57: A ThoughtSpot Data Model.

ThoughtSpot performs the analysis and returns the answer being sought. By "softening" the query process, ThoughtSpot opens up the analytical process to non-technical business professionals. Figure 57 shows a ThoughtSpot Data Model that was created using the original textually-founded medical database and shown here in ThoughtSpot Developer.

As a simple example of the relationship between a ThoughtSpot query and the creation of an answer, the first figure shows Spotter's response to a natural-language user prompt, "What percentage of cases fall under the Dermatology class?"

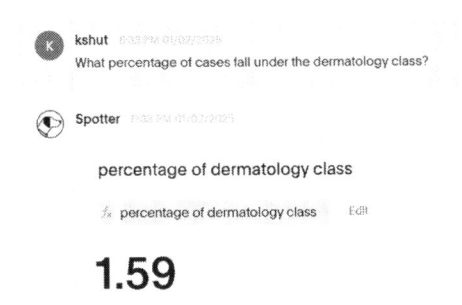

kshut
What percentage of cases fall under the dermatology class?

Spotter

percentage of dermatology class

ƒx percentage of dermatology class   Edit

1.59

Figure 58: "What percentage of cases fall under the Dermatology class?"

Next, we see that ThoughtSpot can also be used with a variety of data sources and models. In this example, Spotter answers a new natural-language user prompt, "How many distinct rootwords are found in the data?"

kshut
How many distinct rootwords are found in the data?

Spotter

Unique Count ROOTWORD

unique count ROOTWORD   Edit

385

Figure 59: "How many distinct rootwords are found in the data?"

120 • MODERNIZING MEDICAL RESEARCH

In addition to giving simple answers that require calculation, ThoughtSpot can produce lists of records, shown here in both traditional and pivot tables.

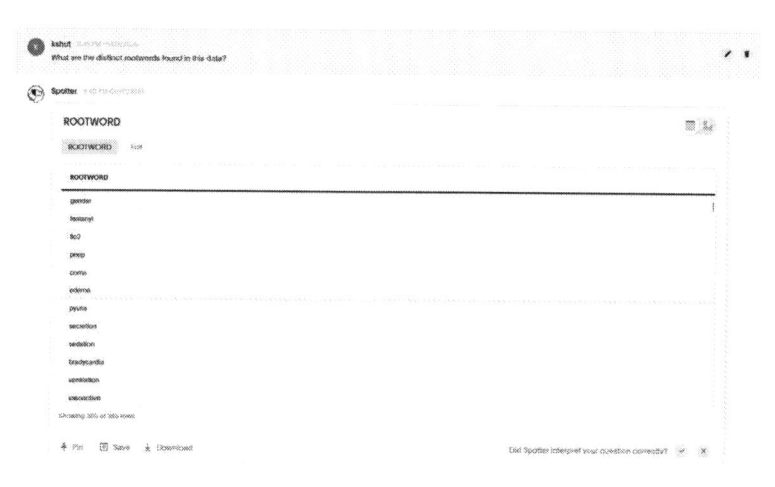

Figure 60: Traditional.

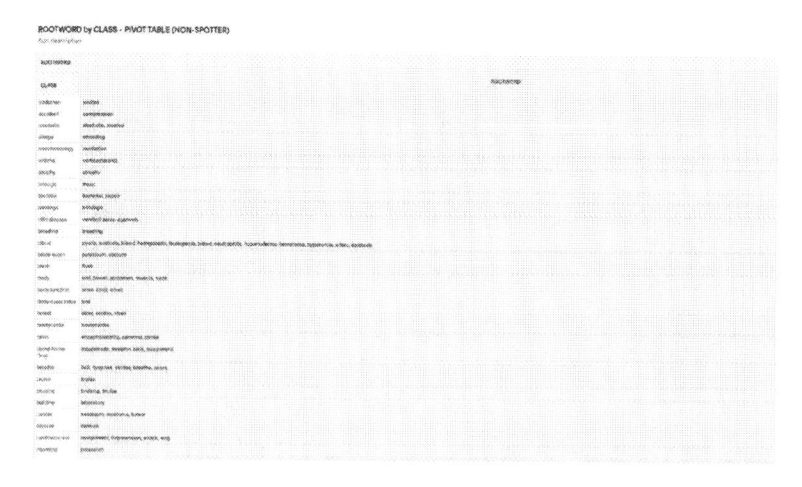

Figure 61: Pivot.

In addition to tabular report results, ThoughtSpot features a rich set of charts and graphs, ranging from traditional bar and line graphs to KPIs, pie and donut charts, waterfall, bubble, scatter, and pareto charts, heatmaps and geomaps, and many more.

Figure 62: A rich set of charts and graphs.

Finally, business professionals can use ThoughtSpot to combine individual prompt responses and query answers into brilliant dashboards, called 'Liveboards', as seen in Figure 63.

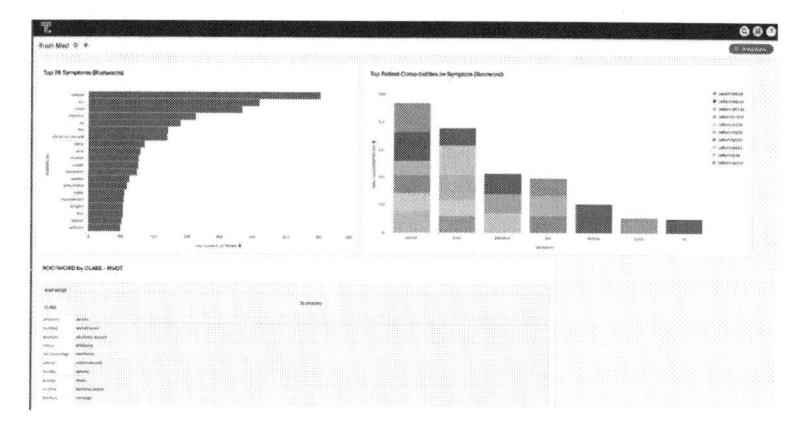

Figure 63: Liveboards.

Knowledge graphs – Neo4j

A different approach to analytics is provided by Neo4j.

Neo4j stores and visualizes data as knowledge graphs. A knowledge graph is a way to store and organize data and data relationships, such that the relationships are stored explicitly (not inferred from metadata like foreign keys). The very structure of a Neo4j database is made for understanding relationships. Unlike some other products, Neo4j supports a dynamic understanding of data.

Furthermore, Neo4j can display those relationships graphically, which helps to uncover hidden patterns in the data.

Neo4j's strength is in storing relationships between data points directly. Storing relationships directly leads to very fast performance when traversing relationships, even when traversing many of them. This enables users to:

- Better understand the context of data by understanding data that is related/connected.

- Use the relationship information to understand or visually represent connections that are difficult in other types of databases; for example, performing contact tracing to understand the spread of an infectious disease.

- Find hidden patterns in data, such as when looking for fraudulent behavior in financial transactions or insurance claims.

The graphical display and the support of dynamic data mean that Neo4j is very well positioned for supporting descriptive and predictive analytics surrounding text.

Neo4j displays different objects (nodes) and the relationships between them. The use of color coding depicts types of nodes. In this graph, a medical researcher can quickly see the possible co-morbidity conditions or current medications (green nodes) for a single patient (orange node).

A different usage of Neo4j is shown where Neo4j connects the data objects that have similar context references. This graph can show where two diverse patient groups share a single node. This is paramount in contact tracing.

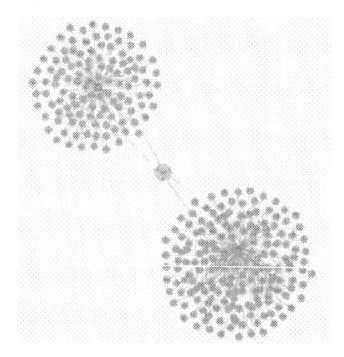

Figure 64: Neo4j.

Figure 65 shows where different relationships exist between different objects. Quite often there are multiple connections between two nodes. Neo4j can represent this with thicker, darker, or multiple connection lines which represent the strength of bonds between nodes.

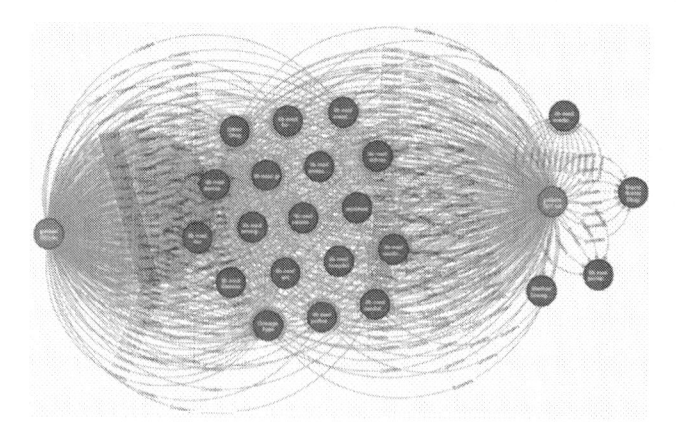

Figure 65: different relationships exist between different objects.

Dashboards – Tableau

A dashboard is a graphical display of the data found in the database. In addition, detailed data and/or filtered detail data can be displayed in a dashboard. A dashboard is made primarily for management, although technical analysts can also use a dashboard.

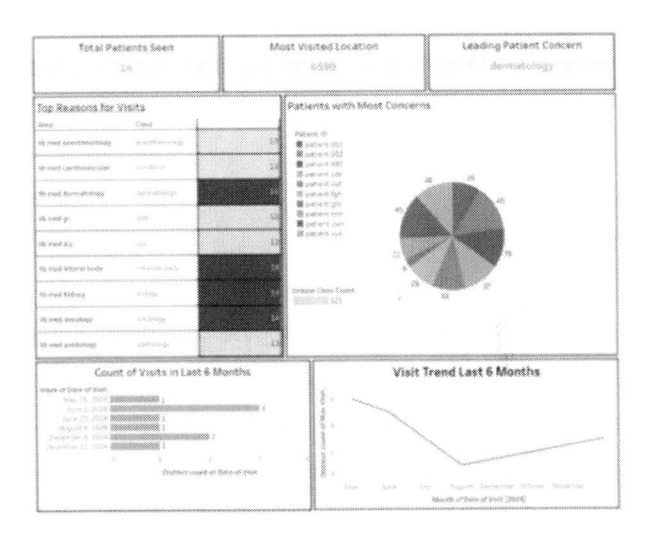

Figure 66: A dashboard.

One of the components of the composite dashboard is the listing of the top ten reasons why a person was placed in the hospital.

126 • MODERNIZING MEDICAL RESEARCH

Figure 67: top ten reasons why a person was placed in the hospital.

Another interesting piece of information is the information relating to customers with the most complaints.

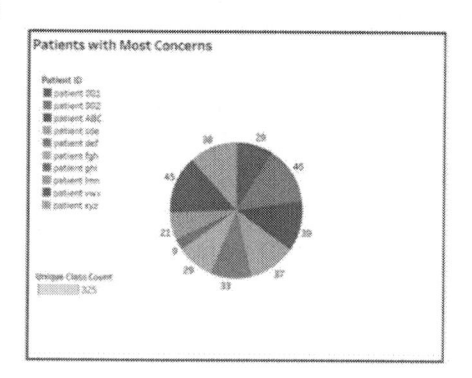

Figure 68: customers with the most complaints.

Yet another useful piece of information is the information about the number of visits made by a patient in the last six months.

ANALYTICS • 127

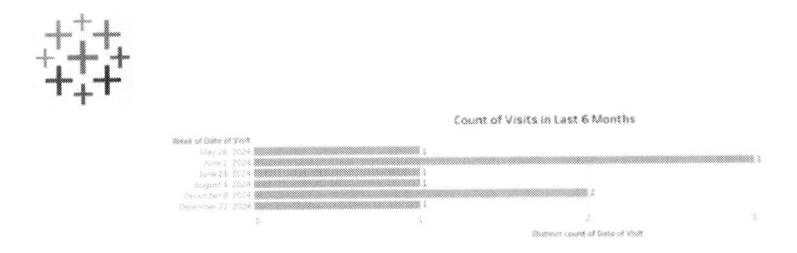

Figure 69: number of visits made by a patient in the last six months.

Another analysis that can be useful is the trend of visits in the past few months, where the number of visits are increasing or decreasing, and at what rate.

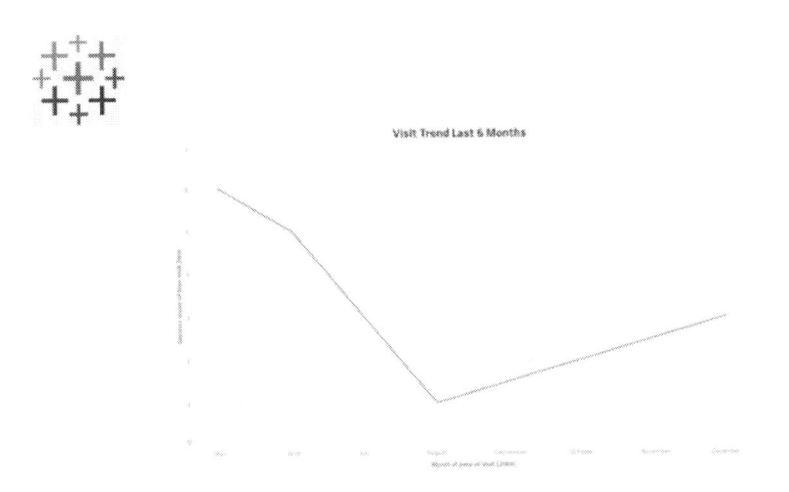

Figure 70: trend of visits in the past few months.

Another analysis can show graphically the number of times each class is found by color and size.

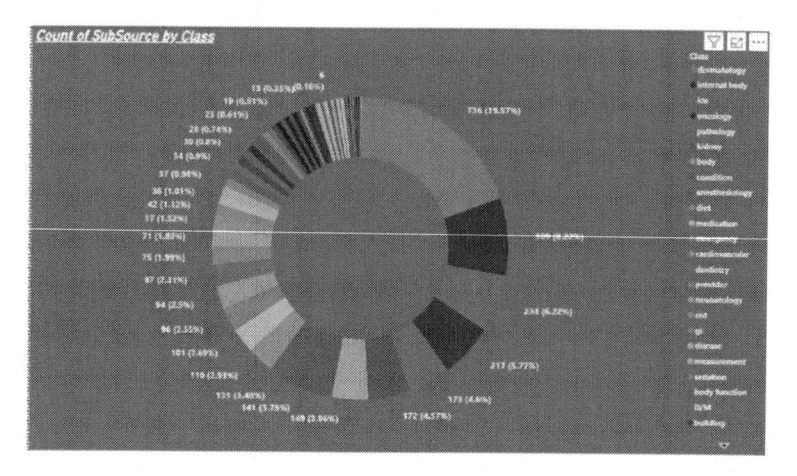

Figure 71: the number of times each class is found by color and size.

Chapter 9

Analytics on Structured and Textual Data

As the world expands its focus from structured data to a combined world of structured and textual data, a question arises: Can we do analytical processing against structured data and textual data simultaneously? It turns out that this is a complex question with a complex answer. The answer is that sometimes we can do combined analytical processing against structured data and textual data, but sometimes we can't do combined analytical processing. There are many facets to this complicated question.

Analytics in the structured environment

Analytics have been done on structured data for many years now. There have been cubes, reports, dashboards, and knowledge graphs. Analytics done on structured data takes many forms: key performance indicators, trend analysis, exception analysis, monthly reports, and so forth. Analytics on structured data is not new.

A typical (simple) structured database contains records with keys and associated attributes. The same structure is repeated over and over for each new entry into the structured database. Typically, a structured database is derived from business transactions, such as the payment of a bill, the purchase of an item, or the making of a reservation.

Analytics on textual data, such as a medical record, is much newer than structured data analytics. It is only since text has been able to be converted to a structured environment efficiently that analytics on text has been able to be done.

There are many forms of analytics on text, such as corelative analytics, voice of the customer analytics, sentiment analysis, pattern analysis, and so forth.

Analytics on both structured and textual data

What is new is the notion that analytics should be able to be done using a combination of structured and textual data simultaneously. Unfortunately, this is a very complex issue that deserves a lengthy and well-thought-out answer. It turns out that this issue is very complex. There are many facets to this proposition.

The database created from raw text, the textual database, looks very different from that created for structured, transaction-based data. The database for text identifies the document, the byte address of the word that has been encountered, and the classification or the context of the word, among other things. This internal structuring of the data is very different from the classical form of a database.

This chapter identifies the issues of doing analytics against structured and textual data at the same time and assesses as to whether a combined analysis of structured and textual data can be done and under what conditions the analysis can be done.

Different organizations of data

The beginning point of the discussion of the analytics that can be done on structured and textual data at the same time is the observation that structured data and textual data are fundamentally different and organized in a fundamentally different manner. Structured data is organized along the lines of records. Each structured record has one or more keys. The keys serve to identify the record uniquely. Each structured record has the same structure as every other structured record. Only the contents of the structured records are different. The keys of the structured records give each record an identity. Usually, the identity is unique. On occasion, the identity of the record only serves to classify the record. The programmer can select a record from the structured database based on the value found in the keys. As an example, suppose there are two structured records:

Ssno – 458-71-1873, name – Bill, dob – July 20 1936
Ssno – 720-90-8156, name – Mary, dob – Aug 16, 1994

In this case, each record can be identified by the data found in the record

The structure of textual data found in a textual database is entirely different. Textual data is organized along the lines of categories or classifications of data, not unique identifiers of data. As such, individual records found in a database whose foundation is text have a unique key that relates only to the document on which the text is found. The only key to the database containing textual data is the source document and the byte address of the word encountered. Multiple records in the textual data environment have the same classification of the word encountered. Both the classification of the word encountered and the word itself may be found many times in the database created for textual data.

As an example, suppose some records come from the textual environment:

Doc ABC, byte 263, tree – pine
Doc BCD, byte 195, tree – pine
Doc ABC, byte 1089, tree – elm

In this case, the text only mentions the trees in the forest, not any particular tree. There is no singular identification of any given tree in the textual database. The mentions in the document are to the tree type, not a particular tree itself. And there may well be multiple mentions of the type of tree in the source document.

This fundamental difference in the basic organization of structured data and textual data makes analytical processing against the two types of data difficult and awkward. However, in some cases, the two different types of data can be integrated so that analytics can be created from both types of data at the same time.

To illustrate this fundamental difference, consider a body of people (such as a political party) versus a description of a forest.

Structured data   Textual data

Bill 37 years old male
Mary 16 years old female
John 87 years old male
Chris 43 years old female
Joe 34 years old male
....

Each record is unique

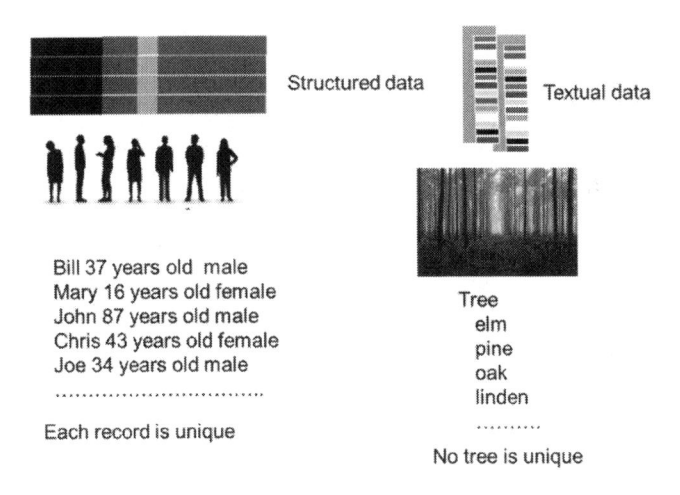

Tree
elm
pine
oak
linden
....
No tree is unique

Figure 72: The merging of data from the structured environment and the textual environment becomes problematic.

Each person in the political party in the structured environment has their own unique identification and defining characteristics.

But when you go to the text about the forest, trees are identified according to their type, but there is no individual identification for each tree.

Intersecting data

To bring these two very different organizations of data together, it is necessary to have some intersection of data between the structured data and the textual data. The connection between the two types of data is created by a common identifier that is shared by both environments.

In some cases, there is such an identifier. In other cases, there is no identifier.

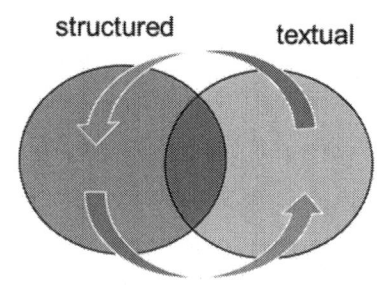

Figure 73: The domains are connected by means of an intersection of data.

If there is in fact an intersection of data then it is possible that the two types of data can be combined. If there is no data on which to connect the structured and the textual environment, then the data cannot be combined to connect the data types. Note that there may be no meaningful data intersection between the two data types. When there is no meaningful intersection of data between the structured and textual data, there can be no meaningful analytics done on the data.

Connectors

If there is an intersection of data between the two types of data, the intersection is formed by the coincidence and orchestration of connectors. In the case where there are connectors, some data in the structured environment relates to some data in the textual environment. The relationship of the data can take many different forms.

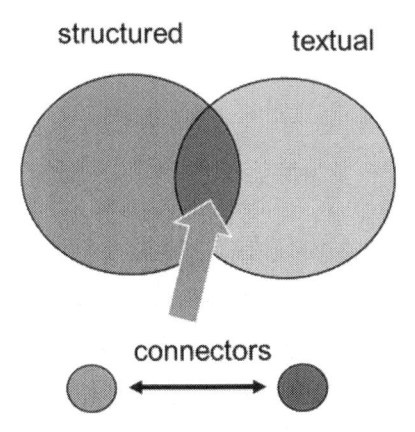

Figure 74: The connection, however it is manifested, is formed by matching connectors that appear in each environment.

Stable/unstable connectors

If there are connectors between the two environments, it is noted that some connectors form a very stable relationship and other connectors form an essentially unstable relationship. An unstable relationship can be called a weak relationship and a stable relationship can be called a strong relationship.

The elements that make a connector relationship weak or strong are the integrity of the relationship itself and the number of times the relationship occurs.

An unstable relationship of connectors might be the connecting of the name, John Smith, in the structured environment to the occurrence of the name J M Smith in the textual environment. In this case, J M Smith may or may not be the same person as John Smith. Stated differently, the integrity of the relationship is in question. This is an example of the instability of a relationship. The instability is caused by the questionable integrity of the relationship itself.

As another simple example, consider the word "Paris" which is found in the structured environment and the textual environment. If all that exists is the word "Paris", it is not clear whether it is Paris, France or Paris, Texas.

On the other hand, if a Social Security number appears in both the structured environment and the textual environment, it is highly likely that the relationship is stable and strong. In this case, the integrity of the relationship is not in question.

The second element in the strength of a relationship is the number of occurrences of the relationship between the two types of data. In some cases, the connection appears very infrequently and in other cases, the relationship occurs frequently.

The greater the number of occurrences, the stronger the relationship. The fewer times the relationship appears, the weaker the relationship.

Types of relationships

There are five types of relationships between structured data and textual data:

- No relationship
- Universal relationship
- Direct relationship
- Indirect relationship
- Classification-based relationship.

No relationship

In the case of no relationship, the structured world and the world depicted by the textual data are so far removed from each other that no meaningful bond can be found. For example, consider the passenger manifest of a cruise line and a description of the oasis in the Sahara desert. The passenger manifest is a collection of structured data. The description of the desert oasis is a verbal description of water in a dry land. In this case, the relationship between a cruise line and an oasis in the Sahara desert is so far removed that there is no meaningful bond between the two worlds. Even if a bond could be found, the bond would be so far fetched that the bond would have no value to the analyst.

Universal relationship

Nearly all data, structured or textual, can be connected by what can be called "universal connectors". The universal connectors are:

- Time
- Geography
- Money (most of the time)

Regardless of what data is being captured, there is always a way to relate time to the data in both the structured and textual environments. In the structured environment, the element of time attached to the data might be the moment of a transaction. The element of time might be the moment of capture of the record. The element of time might be the signing of a contract. One way or the other, structured data always has one (or more) elements of time that can be attached to the structured record.

Text is the same way. You can always attach a moment in time to text. The moment in time may be when the text was stated (if it is text that was spoken.) Or the moment when the text was written. Or published. And so forth. So it is always possible to attach an element of time to both structured and textual data. In some cases, capturing and noting the moment in time is a useful and meaningful thing to do. However, in other cases, merely relating data by time may not be meaningful.

The same considerations apply to geography. Structured transactions always occur geographically somewhere. And text is always created somewhere. And in some cases, geography is a meaningful unifier of the data. In other cases, the geography of the data is not meaningful.

A third universal connector is that of money. In truth, money used as a connector is not truly universal. But money used as a connector often is useful.

In the structured environment, there is almost always some cost or financial factor that can be associated with the data. The textual environment sometimes has a cost or financial factor associated with the data. In other cases, money cannot be reasonably connected to the text in the textual environment.

When a dollar amount can be attached to the data, it may make sense to use money as the unifying characteristic of the data. On the other hand, even when money is the unifying factor, the comparison still may not be useful.

Direct relationship

Another type of connector is that of the direct connector. The direct connector is a connection formed when the same data appears in both the structured and textual environments.

For example, suppose there is a manufacturer that numbers the parts and products created in the manufacturing plant. A new structured list of the products is created each day, and the plant's final output is recorded.

Then, one day, a customer opens their order and finds a defective product. In talking with the customer representative, the customer finds the product number of the product that is defective and relays that to the manufacturer.

In this example, there is a direct connection, product number, between the structured data created by the manufacturer and the customer who finds the product to be defective. This is an example of a direct connection between the structured and textual worlds.

The relationship between the two worlds is very strong. But the number of occurrences is very slight. Because the number of data occurrences is slight, the connection is weak, although it is a very solid one.

ANALYTICS ON STRUCTURED AND TEXTUAL DATA • 141

Indirect relationship

An indirect connector is a connector that relates one type of data to another type of database on an incidental or indirect identification of data. For example, suppose that there is a daily register of a restaurant's revenue in a restaurant chain. Each day, the store reports its revenue to headquarters in a very structured fashion.

Now, suppose a reference to the store appears on the Internet. Yelp is a place where the reference on the Internet might appear. In this case, the demeanor of the Yelp reference might be indirectly connected to the revenue of the store for the day the reference was made. A customer may like his/her visit to the restaurant or may have had a bad experience. In such a fashion, an indirect relationship between types of data can be formed.

connectors

●◄──────►●

Types of connectors
Classifications

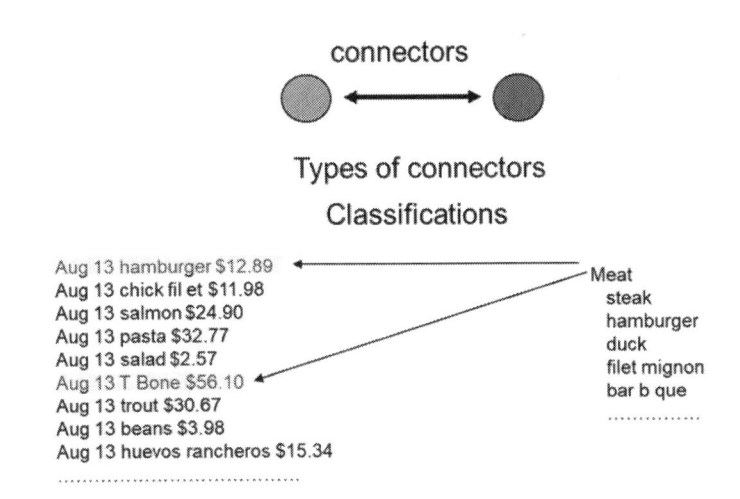

Aug 13 hamburger $12.89   Meat
Aug 13 chick fil et $11.98   steak
Aug 13 salmon $24.90   hamburger
Aug 13 pasta $32.77   duck
Aug 13 salad $2.57   filet mignon
Aug 13 T Bone $56.10   bar b que
Aug 13 trout $30.67   ....
Aug 13 beans $3.98
Aug 13 huevos rancheros $15.34
....

Figure 75: An indirect relationship between types of data.

Classification-based relationship

In the case of the relationship of data formed by classifications, structured data can be subjected to the same classification as textual data.

For example, suppose a restaurant has a daily list of all the dishes ordered that day. This list is a very structured list. The classifications that are used to analyze the textual data can be independently applied to the data found in the structured environment.

For example, the restaurant lists the types of meals that have been served. There is steak, chicken, fish, and so forth. The classifications used to process the textual data can be applied to the meal types that are found in the structured environment. In doing so, a relationship between the two types of data can be created.

Different connections

It is seen then that there are many different ways to connect data from the structured environment to the textual environment. Each of these types of relationships have their advantages and disadvantages.

Universal connections can always be made. But universal connections may not be relevant or meaningful even if they can be created.

Direct relationships can be formed as well. The meaning of the data in a direct relationship is usually very strong, but the relationship may not occur very often.

Indirect relationships can sometimes be created. When an indirect relationship is created, it is usually a strong to moderately strong relationship. However, there is much textual data where there is no basis for such a connection.

Classification relationships can be very strong and useful if the data for such a classification exists. However, there are many cases where no basis for forming the connection exists.

Having looked at the possibilities for connecting structured and textual data, it now becomes obvious that there are many cases where textual data and structured data cannot be combined, as the data for such a foundation simply does not exist. There are cases where a relationship between structured data and textual data has a foundation of data that can be combined. However, that relationship may be weak due to the integrity of the relationship or the infrequency of the occurrence of the relationship. There are cases where a strong and reliable relationship exists between structured data and textual data. In these cases, it is possible to do analytics on the combination of structured and textual data.

An example of blending textual and structured data in analytics

Suppose research needed to be conducted on medications that are used in the treatment of COVID. In particular, the medications Paxlovid and Lagrevio are of interest.

The first step is to limit the boundaries of this fictional study. For the purpose of our example, the geographical location studied is the state of Kansas, and the time frame for the study is 2024.

A structured analysis can be conducted by looking at the prescriptions that have been filled out. This is done by accessing pharmaceutical records which are obtained from pharmacy transactions. A simple analysis shows that in the state of Kansas for 2024, there were 10,350 prescriptions of Paxlovid that were filled and that there were 578 prescriptions of Lagrevio that were filled for Kansas in 2024. The count of the prescriptions is simple enough.

Paxlovid and Lagrevio are usually prescribed together for the treatment of COVID. However, on some occasions, Paxlovid is prescribed independently of COVID for other medical purposes.

Because of this discrepancy, looking at the simple math and declaring the ratio of prescriptions generated by the pharmacies for the usage of Paxlovid and Lagrevio can be very misleading.

The actual prescription activity generated by the doctor is needed to have an accurate understanding of the data. This information is found in the medical records generated by the doctor for the patient. Of course, the medical records are in a textual format, not a structured format.

The medical records are obtained and passed through textual ETL. A database is generated.

Now, the analyst looks for three things in the textual database created by scanning medical records:

- COVID
- Paxlovid
- Lagrevio

The analyst discovers that in Kansas for 2024 that there were 471 mentions of these ingredients collectively in the medical records.

The analyst now knows how many times Paxlovid was prescribed along with Lagrevio. In addition, the analyst knows how many times Paxlovid was prescribed when COVID was not a factor. This last number is created by subtracting the COVID base of Paxlovid prescriptions from the textual medical record data from the total Paxlovid prescriptions from the structured pharmaceutical data. The COVID-related prescriptions number is obtained from textual data and the total prescriptions is obtained from structured information.

The connectors that are used to relate these data together to each other are:

- Paxlovid
- Lagrevio

In such a manner, analysis against textual data combined with structured can be accomplished.

In summary

On occasion, it is desired to connect a database made from textual data to a classical structured database. Sometimes, this connection can be made. On other occasions, this connection cannot be meaningfully made.

If there is an intersection of the two types of data, it is possible to make a connection. If there is no meaningful connection between the two types of data, then it is unlikely that an analysis crossing the types of data that can be made.

Chapter 10

The Analytical Lifecycle

There is a roadmap to doing medical research in an efficient, organized manner using modern data collection and analysis tools. The roadmap steps and details have been discussed in earlier chapters. A summary appears in Figure 76.

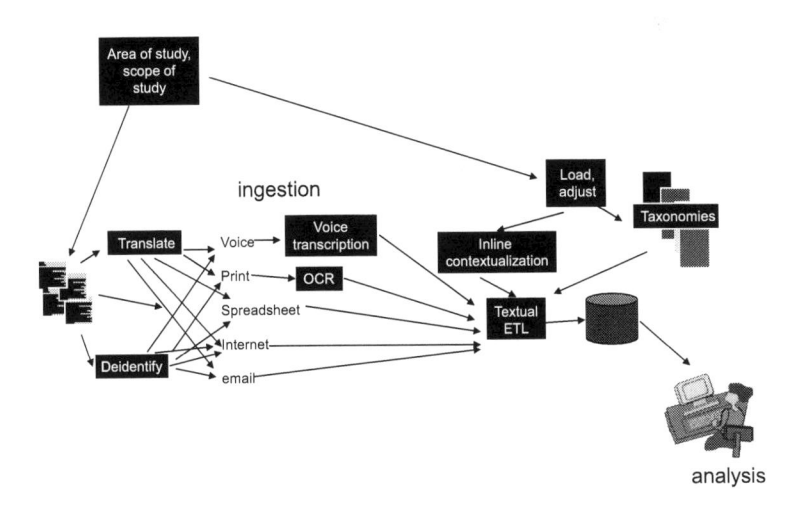

Figure 76: The steps to achieving analysis from raw documents.

A "normal" procedure

The steps through the roadmap can occur in many fashions. However, the "standard" fashion for completing the steps appears in Figure 76.

The first step is determining a general scope and direction for the subject of interest. This scope and direction define what the study is about and what the study hopes to accomplish. The scope and direction do not have to be defined precisely. Indeed, as the analysis proceeds, the scope may be changed, either widened or limited.

The next standard step of the analysis is to prepare the taxonomies and the inline contextualization definitions that are needed, and then the taxonomies and contextualization are loaded into textual ETL. It is normal for the selection of the taxonomies to be in its own iterative process. Certain taxonomies are chosen and then those taxonomies are customized. Then, a few other taxonomies are added, customized, and so forth.

In many regards, taxonomies are like Legos. Many small ones exist and they are combined to create a large taxonomy.

> The taxonomies and the inline contextualization represent the "brains" of the processing of the textual data.

After the taxonomies and the inline contextualization are completed, the next step is to select the medical records and other relevant textual input that will be used in the study. The medical records can come from all sorts of sources: laboratories, doctors' notes, surgical records, EMT, and so forth.

The analyst needs to make sure that all permissions to access the records are granted. If there is limited access to certain records, then the analyst tries to find another source of the records or a substitute for the records to use.

It is normal for the records selection process to be its own iterative process. During the first iteration of the analysis, certain records are selected. On the next iteration, more records are selected, and so forth.

After the records that serve as input to the analysis are identified and selected, we determine the language next. The records must be compatible with the language selected for the taxonomy. It does no good for the medical records to be in Spanish and the taxonomies to be in English, for example. There must be alignment between the language of the records selected and the language of the taxonomy.

Of course, if the language of the records selected is the same as the taxonomy, there is no need for the records to be translated.

After the records not in the taxonomy language are translated into the language used by the taxonomies, the next question is to determine if the records need to be deidentified. Some records will probably be deidentified. Other records may not need to be deidentified. If some or all of the records need to be deidentified, then the records that need to be passed through the deidentification software should be processed.

The net result is a collection of records that are deidentified and in the same language as the language of the taxonomy.

If the records are in the form of voice recordings, they are passed through voice transcription to be placed into an electronic format. If the records are in print, they need to be passed through OCR to be put into electronic format. If the records are on the Internet, then an interface to those records must be acquired. If the records are in email, then the records need to be edited to remove extraneous information.

The next step is to determine how many records will be processed. If needed, the records may be processed on multiple machines. If a single machine is to be used and there are many records, the records can be broken up into physically separate batches and then processed batch by batch.

The records in an electronic format are then loaded into textual ETL and processed.

The database is produced by textual ETL. The analyst should look at the records that have been produced and make sure there are no obvious errors. If obvious errors are discovered, they should be repaired and the text rerun. Because of the likely need to rerun processing through textual ETL, it makes sense to run only a handful of representative records through the first time.

After the analyst is satisfied that the records are being processed successfully, the analyst runs a large batch. Since there is a high likelihood that the first pass through textual ETL will not be successful, it is wise to process only a few records at the outset.

If the records have been broken into different batches to reduce the workload size, either on a single machine or on multiple machines, the output data is collected from the processing of multiple batches and is collected into a single batch. The resultant database is then turned over to the analyst for analytical processing and analysis.

Flexibility

The order of the processes that have been described is not set in stone. There is actually a lot of flexibility in the order of steps of execution of the analytical process. The only thing set in stone is that the text needs to be in an electronic format and that the taxonomies and inline contextualization must be set before running textual ETL. For example, the source documents can be gathered and processed independently into an electronic state before selecting and analyzing the taxonomies and the inline contextualization.

Of course, the taxonomies must be defined and loaded before processing on textual ETL can proceed. But the collection and processing of the source documents do not have to be done until after all the taxonomy analysis has been done.

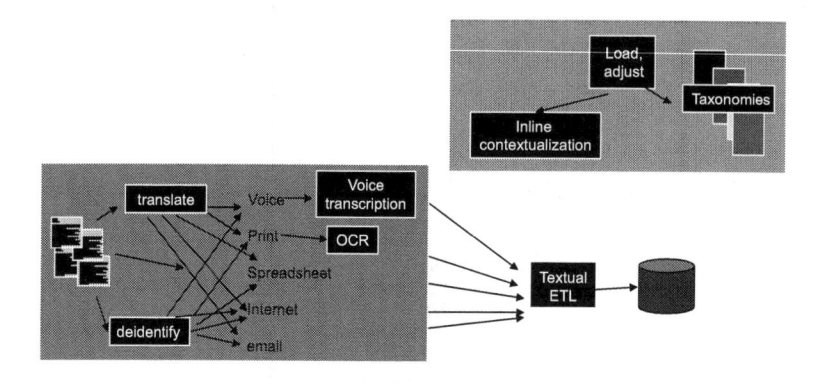

Figure 77: The activities in the two grey rectangles can be done independently.

Length of time

How long do each of these steps of analysis take? It depends. The variable most affecting the time required for processing is whether a step has automated support and whether a step already has intellectual property that can be used in place. If a step has automated support and/or intellectual property exists that can be used, the processing is done quickly. But if a step has to be done manually and/or if new intellectual property must be created, then the step will take longer.

In some cases, such support exists. Support does not exist in other cases and must be done by hand. The good news is that many steps have automated support and intellectual property that can be used as is. For example, automated translation across language facilities exists on the Internet and can be done in a matter of seconds. Or automated textual ETL exists and can process records as fast as desired.

On the other hand, the selection of medical records for inclusion into the study must be done by hand. And the determination of the scope and the direction of the analysis must also be done by hand.

The loading of taxonomies is a very automated process and can be done quickly, even for the largest collection of taxonomies.

If the taxonomy must be created from scratch, it may take a week to create a new one. However, if the taxonomy needed is in the standard taxonomy library, selecting and loading the existing taxonomy takes only seconds. If extensive customization is needed for a taxonomy, the customization may take an hour or two.

For even the most complicated data, inline contextualization usually only takes an hour or two.

The selection and authentication of the permission to use the documents that have been selected is a manual process. This process is the most variable and problematic of all the steps. The process of selection and authorization may take minutes. The step may take months. It all depends on the nature and volume of the documents that are needed for the study.

In the worst case, it may turn out that the documents that are needed are simply not available. In this case, the documents may be able to be provided by another source. Or there may be very similar documents that can be used that are available.

If the documents need to be translated into another language or if the documents need to be deidentified, this process takes only a short amount of time because both of those processes have been automated.

In the same vein, if the documents need to go through voice transcription or OCR, these processes are problematic because they have been automated for a long time and are mature technologies.

Speed of textual ETL

Once the text from the documents is in the form of electronic text, the text is ready to be processed by textual ETL. The speed of textual ETL processing depends entirely on the number of machines used for the processing. The speed can be calculated as:

Time (in seconds) = pages of documents/ (3 pages per second x number of machines)

Note that the measurement is made in terms of number of pages. A document or medical record may have any number of pages.

As a rule, the biggest factor in the processing of a study depends on the number of documents processed and the size of those documents.

For a medium-sized study, the entire study can be done in as little as three days.

After the study is completed and after the analysis is done, the study is reimagined. The analyst reflects on what was learned and what is yet to learn.

The reimagination of the study occurs because insights will have been gained in the first iteration of the study. Those insights normally raise more questions than answers. Typical insights might be:

- Include a different kind of data into the study.
- Include a different class of activity in the study.
- Include data from a previous time and/or location in the study.
- Change the way some data is interpreted in the study.

The analyst and the director of the study can change anything and everything, including the direction of the study. This reimagining of the study is normal and usually essential. It almost never happens that the first iteration of the study tells the researcher everything that is needed.

Attitude

There are many reasons why a review and reconsider proposition occurs at the end of an analysis iteration. The primary reason for review and reconsideration is that the analyst who instigated the study operates in a mode of, "Give me what I say I want, then I can tell you what I really want."

The originating analyst operates in a mode of discovery and exploration. The analyst does not know what is useful and interesting until the analyst can see the interacting factors. The first and second iterations of analysis open up the eyes of the analyst as to what the possibilities are. Once the analyst starts to understand what the possibilities are, the analyst now has a better idea of what to explore further.

Reconsidering the study

So, where does a reconsideration of the parameters of a study start? The answer is that it can start with any of several points:

- The taxonomies and/or the inline contextualization can be reestablished.
- The source documents can be expanded (or shrunk).
- The actual analysis can be adjusted.
- Even the scope and the direction of the study can be changed.

And, of course, all of these factors can be changed. There is nothing to say that only one aspect of the study can be changed.

If taxonomies, inline contextualization, or the study's scope is changed, reprocessing the raw text is probably necessary. However, if all that is changed is the source documents, then it is very unlikely that a reprocess must take place. Even where a reprocess needs to occur, it is likely that much of the data that has been processed in an existing iteration will still be useful and insightful. The analytical process that has been described is streamlined compared to previous methods and approaches. The process that is described is very fast. The speed of the analytical approach enables the research organization to do fast iterations of analysis. The speed of the process enables the organization to have great freedom in conducting a study. And, of course, the more freedom the analyst has, the greater the chances for a successful analysis.

In summary

The nature of analysis is to explore the unknown. This means that the analyst does not know:

- The number of iterations of analysis
- How long the analysis will take
- The cost of the analysis
- Whether there will be any final outcome of the analysis.

In many ways, studying is an adventure. The final outcome will come when it comes, and you will recognize it when it appears.

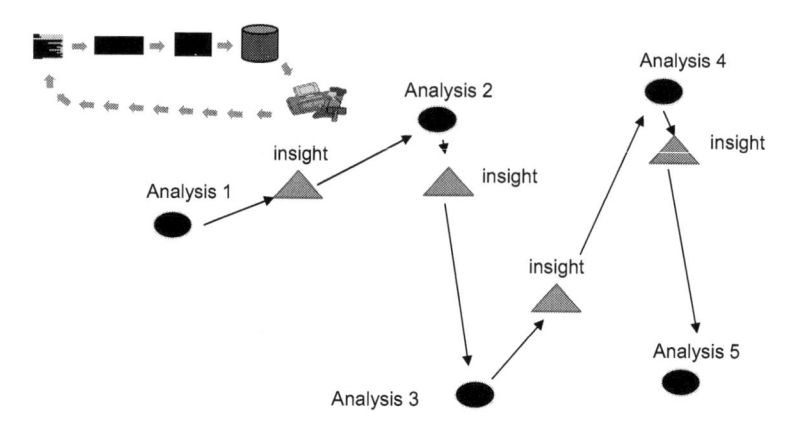

Figure 78: The random path of analysis.

An interesting observation is that each iteration of analysis builds on the previous level of analysis. Even in the case where there is no result of an iteration of analysis, the analyst knows where not to look for the next iteration. In most cases, there is at least some insight that results from an iteration of analysis, even if the insight is not the one the analysts are looking for.

Raw analysis proceeds by trial and error. That is the nature of exploration. Being able to complete iterations of analysis greatly enhances the trial and error process.

As in most adventures in life, taking the first step is the most difficult part. Having a roadmap and technology that supports the roadmap allows the first step to be taken with confidence.

Index

acronyms, 36, 71, 72
Advil, 70
analysis, 15, 17, 18, 19, 20, 21, 22, 23, 24, 25, 32, 37, 40, 41, 43, 44, 48, 51, 55, 59, 61, 64, 65, 68, 72, 74, 75, 76, 87, 88, 89, 92, 93, 94, 97, 98, 99, 104, 105, 106, 107, 108, 109, 110, 113, 114, 116, 118, 127, 130, 131, 144, 146, 147, 148, 149, 151, 152, 153, 155, 156, 157, 158
analyst, 2, 15, 17, 18, 20, 21, 22, 23, 24, 26, 27, 39, 40, 41, 45, 49, 50, 55, 60, 64, 65, 70, 71, 72, 73, 74, 75, 76, 79, 82, 83, 85, 88, 92, 97, 98, 104, 106, 116, 138, 145, 149, 150, 151, 155, 156, 157, 158
analytic processing, 19
analytics, 5, 12, 16, 17, 57, 63, 65, 76, 107, 108, 122, 123, 130, 131, 133, 135, 143
Aspirin, 70
Bertillon, Jacques, 90
cancer, 10

cardiologist, 72
classifications, 36, 132, 142
clinical study, 55
common language, 68
connectors, 135, 136, 138, 146
correlation, 95, 98, 100, 101, 102, 103, 104
COVID, 10, 91, 92, 103, 104, 144, 145
CPT. See Current Procedural Terminology
Current Procedural Terminology, 90
data professionals, 1
databases, 2, 14, 81, 86, 109, 114, 123
Datavox, 78, 79, 80, 81, 82
DB2, 81
decision maker, 17
deidentification, 38, 150
diabetes, 10
diagnostics, 9
diastolic, 74
direct connector, 140
disease, 8, 11, 28, 36, 115, 116, 123

doctor, 8, 9, 10, 23, 24, 32, 42, 54, 56, 67, 68, 72, 87, 106, 107, 145
drill-across approach, 99
drill-down approach, 98
emails, 50
encoded, 66
ETL. See Extract, Transform, and Load
Excel, 112, 116
Extract, Transform, and Load, 16
formats, 12, 45, 46, 51, 75
furosemide, 64, 75
GenAI. See Generative Artificial Intelligence
Generative Artificial Intelligence, 118
healthcare provider, 32
HIPAA, 3, 38, 51
homograph, 72, 73
ICD-10. See International Classifications of Diseases' tenth revision
indirect connector, 141
ingesting text, 63
inline contextualization, 148, 149, 151, 153, 156, 157
International Classifications of Diseases' tenth revision, 90

Internet, 45, 46, 47, 51, 141, 150, 153
knowledge graphs, 122, 130
Lagrevio, 144, 145, 146
Lasix, 64, 75
laws, 3, 37, 38, 51, 90
lisinopril, 32
measurement, 68, 73, 75, 102, 155
media, 13, 39, 45, 51
medical journals, 53, 54, 59
medical practices, 1
medical professionals, 1, 91
medical records, 2, 3, 7, 8, 9, 11, 12, 13, 14, 15, 16, 17, 22, 24, 25, 26, 37, 38, 39, 40, 41, 42, 43, 44, 45, 46, 47, 48, 49, 50, 51, 53, 54, 55, 56, 57, 63, 64, 65, 77, 78, 79, 80, 83, 87, 88, 89, 98, 104, 105, 106, 107, 145, 149, 153
medical research, 1, 2, 10, 14, 24, 26, 37, 50, 53, 56, 57, 59, 65, 147
Medicare, 90
Neo4j, 112, 122, 123, 124
non-linear approach, 98
nurse, 9
OCR, 47, 48, 49, 150, 154
ontology, 25, 26, 34, 35, 36
Oracle, 81

INDEX • 161

parallel processing, 44
patient records, 24, 54, 103
patient vital signs, 9
Paxlovid, 144, 145, 146
Pearson coefficient matrix, 102, 103, 104
pivot tables, 116, 117, 120
prescribed medications, 9
print, 2, 47, 49, 51, 150
procedures, 7, 8, 9, 75, 79
scatter diagram, 99, 100
Social Security number, 38, 51, 69, 83, 136
speed, 20, 21, 24, 59, 76, 80, 104, 105, 154, 157
spelling, 70
spreadsheets, 48, 49, 51, 116
SQL Server, 81
structured, 15, 23, 42, 69, 109, 110, 111, 112, 114, 129, 130, 131, 132, 133, 134, 135, 136, 137, 138, 139, 140, 141, 142, 143, 144, 145, 146
surgery, 32, 42, 67
symptoms, 8, 9
systolic, 74
taxonomy, 25, 26, 27, 28, 29, 30, 31, 32, 33, 34, 35, 36, 81, 84, 85, 148, 149, 150, 152, 153

Teradata, 81
text, 2, 3, 13, 14, 15, 16, 17, 19, 20, 21, 22, 24, 25, 26, 27, 28, 29, 30, 31, 32, 33, 34, 35, 36, 37, 39, 40, 43, 46, 47, 48, 49, 50, 51, 53, 54, 55, 57, 58, 59, 60, 61, 63, 65, 66, 67, 68, 71, 74, 76, 80, 85, 86, 105, 107, 110, 111, 115, 123, 130, 131, 132, 133, 134, 139, 150, 151, 154, 157
textual ETL, 16, 25, 26, 27, 30, 31, 32, 34, 43, 44, 45, 49, 61, 66, 77, 78, 79, 80, 84, 85, 86, 105, 145, 148, 150, 151, 152, 153, 154
textual-based database, 111, 112, 114
ThoughtSpot, 112, 118, 119, 120, 121
Tylenol, 70, 116
universal, 138, 139, 143
unstructured, 14, 15
voice transcription, 49, 50, 150, 154
WHO. See World Health Organization
World Health Organization, 90
x-ray, 39

Made in the USA
Columbia, SC
03 April 2025